Thingamajigs
and
Whatchamacallits

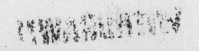

Thingamajigs and Whatchamacallits

~~~~~~~~~~~~~~~~~~~~~~~~

UNFAMILIAR TERMS
FOR FAMILIAR THINGS

~~~~~~~~~~~~~~~~~~~~~~~~

Rod L. Evans, Ph.D.

A PERIGEE BOOK

A PERIGEE BOOK
Published by the Penguin Group
Penguin Group (USA) Inc.
375 Hudson Street, New York, New York 10014, USA

Penguin Group (Canada), 90 Eglinton Avenue East, Suite 700, Toronto,
Ontario M4P 2Y3, Canada (a division of Pearson Penguin Canada Inc.) *
Penguin Books Ltd., 80 Strand, London WC2R 0RL, England * Penguin Group
Ireland, 25 St. Stephen's Green, Dublin 2, Ireland (a division of Penguin Books
Ltd.) * Penguin Group (Australia), 250 Camberwell Road, Camberwell, Victoria
3124, Australia (a division of Pearson Australia Group Pty. Ltd.) * Penguin Books
India Pvt. Ltd., 11 Community Centre, Panchsheel Park, New Delhi—110 017,
India * Penguin Group (NZ), 67 Apollo Drive, Rosedale, Auckland
0632, New Zealand (a division of Pearson New Zealand Ltd.) * Penguin Books
(South Africa) (Pty.) Ltd., 24 Sturdee Avenue, Rosebank, Johannesburg 2196,
South Africa

Penguin Books Ltd., Registered Offices: 80 Strand, London WC2R 0RL, England

While the author has made every effort to provide accurate telephone numbers
and Internet addresses at the time of publication, neither the publisher nor the
author assumes any responsibility for errors or for changes that occur after
publication. Further, the publisher does not have any control over and does not
assume any responsibility for author or third-party websites or their content.

First edition: June 2011

Library of Congress Cataloging-in-Publication Data

Evans, Rod L., 1956–
   Thingamajigs and whatchamacallits : unfamiliar terms for familiar things /
Rod L. Evans.— 1st ed.
     p.   cm.
   Includes bibliographical references.
   ISBN 978-0-399-53672-4
   1. Vocabulary.   2. English language—Glossaries, vocabularies, etc.   I. Title.
PE1449.E937 2011
   428.1—dc22   2010054225

PRINTED IN THE UNITED STATES OF AMERICA

10   9   8   7   6   5   4   3   2   1

ACKNOWLEDGMENTS

My deep thanks go to my literary agents, Sheree Bykofsky and Janet Rosen; my excellent editor at Perigee, Meg Leder; the talented freelance copyeditor, Candace Levy; my friends Rob Stewart and Justin Gruver, who helped edit the typescript; and my good friend and extraordinary administrative assistant, known for her extraordinary word-processing skills, Robin Hudgins. This book has been enriched by the hard work of many people. I am grateful.

CONTENTS

INTRODUCTION

We English speakers are heirs to a rich treasure, a language that has so freely borrowed from other languages as to contain more than one million words. Did you ever wonder, for example, what the plastic tips at the end of shoelaces are called? They're aglets. How about the wiggly lines in comic strips to indicate something that is moving? They're agitrons. This dictionary contains unfamiliar but technically correct terms for whatchamacallits, doohickeys, and thingamajigs. Nearly every entry is in at least one unabridged dictionary, though a handful of the entries are recent slang (such as *Googlegänger*, a person who you have found out through a Google search has your same name).

This book is devoted to giving the technically correct though usually unfamiliar words for familiar things. Sometimes its entries are obscure, such as *diastema* (the gap between Madonna's two front teeth) and *philtrum* (the vertical indentation between the upper lip and the nose). At other times, what is obscure is not so much the entry itself as one of its meanings, as when the word *saddle* describes the upper hinge of a matchbook, or when the word *crown* describes the horizontal part of a paper staple.

The entries in this dictionary include not only unfamiliar words for familiar physical objects but also unfamiliar words for familiar ideas, beliefs, and practices. Accordingly, you'll find *theodicy*, describing the theological enterprise of attempting to vindicate a belief in God and God's goodness in the face of evil. Similarly, the book contains *psilanthropist*, describing a person who doesn't believe in Jesus' divinity. Presumably, nearly all *psilanthropists* are unaware that they have a special name, the main component of which literally means "merely human."

Although many people know that the glass protecting a salad bar is a *sneeze guard*, fewer people know that the horizontal bars that lock and unlock exit doors are sometimes called *panic bars*, or that the dependent class (if clause) in conditional sentences is called a *protasis*, as in "My medical insurance premiums will rise *if the 2010 medical reform passed by Congress isn't repealed or declared unconstitutional*."

A Note About Organization

The entries are arranged alphabetically under subjects, such as "Anatomy," "Clothing," and "Eyewear."

A Note About the Definitions

Sometimes the entries will contain more than one definition. More often, the entries will contain only one definition, either the most popular or the one that is most interesting, at least according to the author.

A Note About Parts of Speech

Note that most of the entries are nouns (indicated by *n.*) or adjectives (*adj.*), though some are verbs (*v.* or *imp.* for "imperative") or adverbs (*adv.*). Most of the entries belong to only one part of speech, but some can function as, say, nouns or verbs. Because many of the entries carry multiple meanings, it is possible that this dictionary contains the most popular meaning of a term when it occurs as a noun or a verb but does not contain other meanings of that term when it functions in other parts of speech. The sentence illustrating the meaning will use the word according to the part of speech ascribed to it in the dictionary.

A Note About Word Origins

The dictionary contains a brief explanation of the meanings and origins of the roots of words, not a complete etymological analysis. When a word can be traced through several languages, often only the oldest source will be listed, especially when that source is Greek or Latin.

A Note About Pronunciation

Pronunciations are provided for words that may give people difficulty but not for words whose pronunciations are obvious.

Pronunciation Key

VOWEL SOUNDS
   A, a—pat, pack, mass
   AH, ah—spa, father, pod
   AHR, ahr—car, mar, farm
   AIR, air—pair, rare, bear
   AY, ay—pay, wait, fame
   AW, aw—raw, mall, walk
   E, e—yes, bet, pep
   EE, ee—see, meat, pea

EER, eer—ear, beer, near
I, i—in, pit, nip
Y, y and EYE, eye—my, rice, pie

Note: Y is used in combination with other letters to form a syllable: *RYT-lee* (rightly). *EYE* is used when this sound by itself forms a syllable: *EYE-land* (island).

OH, oh—tow, sew, moat
OO, oo—to, booze, mule
OR, or—core, poor, war
OOR, oor—tour, lure, pure
OY, oy—oil, coin, soy
UH, uh—pup, dull, sum
UU, uu—pull, wood, could

CONSONANT SOUNDS
B, b—ball, cob, bubble
CH, ch—chap, patch, reach
D, d—dig, dad, mud
F, f—fit, affect, laugh
G, g—got, rig, Gus
H, h—hat, hop, hint
J, j—job, magic, cage
K, k—kind, cup, rake
L, l—leg, also, fell
'l—battle, apple, turtle
M, m—mug, drum, gem
'm—chasm, prism, sarcasm
N, n—no, knap, bend
'n—rotten, hidden, treason
NG, ng—ring, anger, sank
P, p—pop, pepper, pin

R, r—rag, large, mar
S, s—sat, mask, gas
SH, sh—she, bush, notion
T, t—tip, butter, mist
TH, th—thin, nothing, thirst
<u>TH, th</u>—their, this, mother
V, v—vet, Steve, give
W, w—well, wave, flower
Y, y—yet, you, layer

Note: (Y), (y) indicates that some speakers employ the Y sound of *you* and others do not: N(Y)OO (new); D(Y)OO-tee (duty); uh-ST(Y)OOT (astute)

Z, z—zoo, glaze, please

STRESS/ACCENT

- Syllables are separated by a hyphen (-).
- Syllables printed in CAPITAL letters are stressed.
- Syllables printed in small (lowercase) letters are not stressed.
- Words of one syllable are printed in CAPITAL letters.
- Words of more than two syllables that have primary and secondary stress are transcribed in the following manner: The syllable with secondary stress is printed in CAPITALS, and the syllable with primary stress is printed in **BOLDFACE CAPITALS**: AHK-tuh-**THORP** (octothorpe).

ANATOMY

ALAE (AY-lee): *n.* from Latin *ala* (wing, armpit, side apartment): the fleshy bulbs on each side of the nose.

"Everything about W. C. Fields's body was bulbous, including the **alae** of his nose."

ANORCHOUS (an-ORK-us): *adj.* from Greek *anorchos*, from Greek *an-* (without) and *orchis* (testicle): without testicles.

"Eunuchs have been trusted around men's wives because **anorchous** men are often unthreatening."

AXILLARY (AK-suh-LAIR-ee): *n.* from Latin *axilla* (armpit, crotch): pertaining to the armpit.

"Because of Melvin's **axillary** odor, we asked him to use an antiperspirant."

CALLIPYGIAN (KAL-i-**PIJ**-ee-in): *adj.* from Greek *kallipygos*, from *kalli-* (beautiful) and *pygē* (buttocks): having shapely buttocks.

"The feminist asked the **callipygian** woman whether she'd like to be remembered for her buns or for her mind and heart."

CANTHUS: *n.* the point at each end of each eye where the upper and lower lids meet.

"Sometimes a surgeon will intentionally cut a **canthus** to release excessive orbital pressure caused by infection."

COLUMELLA (KOL-yuh-MEL-uh): *n.* from Latin *columella* (small column): the fleshy part of the nose, just above the lip, that separates the nostrils.

"The young boy got some chocolate frosting on his **columella** from eating the cake."

CREMAINS (kri-MAYNZ): *n.* from blend of *cremate* and *remains*: the ashes of a cremated body.

"Because Arthur was a sailor, he had asked that Rachel, his daughter, spread his **cremains** in the ocean."

DACTYLION (dak-TIL-ee-UHN): *n.* from Greek *daktylos* (finger) and English *-ion* (diminutive suffix): the tip of the middle finger.

"My right **dactylion** was sore from doing a great deal of writing."

DORSUM: *n.* from Latin *dorsum* (back, slope of a hill): the back of the tongue.

"The boxer injured his **dorsum** when he was struck in the mouth."

FRENULUM (FREN-yuh-luhm): *n.* from Latin *frenum* (bridle): the thin connecting fold of membrane extending from the floor of the mouth to the midline of the underside of the tongue.

"When the **frenulum** under the tongue is abnormally short, it can stop the tongue from poking out of the lips, causing a person to be literally tongue-tied."

GLABELLA (gluh-BEL-uh): *n.* from Latin, feminine of *glabellus* (hairless), from *glaber* (bald): the smooth area between the eyebrows just above the nose.

"When I studied meditation, I was told to focus on my **glabella**, where the third eye is said to be."

GLUTEAL CREASE: *n.* the fold or horizontal groove marking the lower limit of the buttocks, where the lower buttocks meet the upper leg.

"Even people with little body fat have **gluteal creases**, right where the upper leg meets the buttocks."

GNATHION (NAY-thee-ahn): *n.* from Greek *gnathos* (jaw): the lowest point on the midline of the lower jaw: the tip of the chin.

"A solid right hook to Ray's **gnathion** was the knock-out punch."

HALLUX: *n.* the big toe.

"I stubbed my **hallux** on the foot of the table."

INTERGLUTEAL CLEFT: *n.* butt crack.

"The young man was not hired for the job because his droopy pants revealed his **intergluteal cleft**."

LACRIMAL CARUNCLE: *n.* the small, reddish, fleshy protuberance at the medial corner of each eye containing modified sebaceous and sweat glands.

"When I woke up, I noticed a yellowish crust in my **lacrimal caruncles**."

LUNULA (LOON-yuh-luh): *n.* from Latin *lunula*, diminutive of *luna* (Moon): the half-moon or crescent-shaped pale area at the base of a fingernail or toenail.

"On Jodi's little finger, her cuticle obscured the **lunula**."

MINIMUS (MIN-uh-muhs): *n.* from Latin *minimus* (smallest, least): the little finger or toe.

"The young man had to withdraw from the arm-wrestling competition because he had injured the **minimus** of his right hand."

MORTON'S TOE: *n.* the condition in which the first metatarsal, the toe adjacent to the big toe (*see* HALLUX), is longer than the big toe.

"People with **Morton's toe** can experience discomfort from shoes that aren't designed to accommodate the longer second toe."

OCCIPUT (AHK-suh-put, AHK-suh-puht): *n.* from Latin *occiput-*, from *ob-* (against) and *caput* (head): the back part of the head or skull.

"When Jason was rubbing the back of his head, he told us that a racquetball had struck his **occiput**."

OLECRANON (oh-LEK-ruh-nahn): *n.* from Greek *ōlekranon*, from *ōlenē* (elbow) and *kranion* (head, skull): the bony tip of the elbow.

"Although people may call the **olecranon** the funny bone, the bony prominence is actually the end of the ulna, one of the two forearm bones."

OPHRYON (AHF-ree-UHN): *n.* from Greek *ophrys* (brow, eyebrow): the space between the eyebrows on a line with the top of the eye sockets (*see* GLABELLA).

"The **ophryon** is in the brow just above the eye socket and the smooth prominence of the forehead between the eyebrows."

OPISTHENAR (uh-PIS-thuh-NAHR): *n.* the back of the hand, opposite the palm.

"Because Sheila had cold eczema and spent hours outside in winter without gloves, her **opisthenar** was dry, pink, and sore."

PENIAL (PEE-nee-UHL): *n.* of or relating to the penis.

"The Sunday school principal suspended the boy for drawing **penial** diagrams on the chalkboard."

PEOTOMY: *n.* amputation of the penis.

"Lorena Bobbit's **peotomy** on her then-husband Dwayne Bobbit made many men squirm, though Mr. Bobbit recovered enough to later make a porn movie."

PHILTRUM (FIL-trum): *n.* from Greek *philtron* (philter, charm, dimple in the upper lip): the vertical groove on the median line of the upper lip.

"Both Charlie Chaplin and Hitler had mustaches covering only their **philtrums**."

PINNA: *n.* from Latin *pinna* (feather, wing): the largely cartilaginous projecting portion of the external ear.

"The **pinna** of the ear collects sound by acting as a funnel, amplifying the sound and directing it to the auditory canal."

POPLITEAL (pahp-LIT-ee-uhl): *adj.* pertaining to the hollow area behind the knee.

"Whenever I wore shorts during the summers on Chincoteague Island in Virginia, I'd suffer mosquito bites in the **popliteal** areas of my legs."

PROGNATHOUS (PRAHG-nuh-thuhs): *adj.* from Latin *pro-* (before, forward, in front of) and New Latin *-gnathus*, from Greek *gnathos* (jaw): having jaws projecting beyond the upper part of one's face, like Popeye the Sailor Man.

"**Prognathous** jaws can result in malocclusion (including overbite)."

PURLICUE: *n.* the space between the thumb and extended forefinger.

"Because I received a paper cut in my right **purlicue**, I had trouble shaking people's hands."

RASCETA (ruh-SET-uh): *n. pl.* from Medieval Latin *raseta*, from Arabic *rāhah* (palm of the hand): creases on the inside of the wrist.

"Regardless of one's age, **rasceta** are normal on the wrist."

SEPTUM (SEP-tuhm): *n.* from Latin *saeptum* (partition): a dividing wall in an animal or a plant.

"The partition between your nostrils is an example of a **septum**."

THENAR (THEE-nahr): *n.* from Greek *thenar* (palm of the hand): the fleshy pad on the palm of the hand at the base of the thumb.

"When performing bench presses, Matt accidentally pinched his **thenar**."

TRAGUS (TRAY-guhs): *n.* from New Latin, from Greek *tragos* (goat, hairy part of the ear): the fleshy bump (skin-covered cartilage) in front of the external opening of the ear cavity.

"The young woman had earrings in her right ear lobe and right **tragus**."

UVULA (YOOV-yuh-luh): *n.* from Medieval Latin, diminutive of Latin *uva* (grape): the fleshy lobe that hangs down from the back of the mouth.

"Millions of kids mistakenly think that the **uvula** is their tonsils."

VIBRISSAE (vy-BRIS-ee): *n.* from Latin *vibrissae* (hairs in the nostrils), probably from *vibrare* (to shake, vibrate): the whiskers of a cat.

"The cat's **vibrissae** helped it maintain a sense of balance and navigate narrow pathways."

~~~~~~

ANIMALS IN GROUPS

~~~~~~

BASK: *n.* a group of crocodiles, which can also come in *floats*.

"We knew that we had run into a **bask** of crocodiles rather than a CONGREGATION (*see*) of alligators because of their tapered snouts."

BLOAT: *n.* a group of hippos.

"When we saw a **bloat** of hippos in Africa, our biology professor told us that DNA and other evidence seem to indicate that the closest living relatives to hippos aren't pigs but cetaceans, such as whales and porpoises."

BOUQUET: *n.* a group of pheasants *in take-off*.

"Dick shot at a pheasant in a **bouquet** as the pheasant was released from captivity."

BUSINESS: *n.* a group of ferrets.

"It is difficult to keep track of even one ferret, much less a **business** of them."

CACKLE: *n.* a group of hyenas.

"In Kenya, we saw a **cackle** of hyenas feeding on a zebra carcass."

CLOUD: *n.* a group of bats, which can also come in *colonies*.

"At dusk, the young children became frightened by a **cloud** of bats."

CLOWDER: *n.* a group of domestic cats, which can also come in *clutters*, *pounces*, and *glarings* (especially when the cats are uncertain of one another).

"At the animal shelter, we saw a **clowder** of cats playing."

CLUSTER: *n.* a group of spiders, which can also come in *clutters*.

"Running into a web and a **cluster** of spiders frightened the young boy."

COALITION: *n.* a group of cheetahs.

"We thought that we had run into leopards until we saw the animals go from zero to sixty miles per hour to pursue prey; we then knew we had seen a **coalition** of cheetahs."

CONGREGATION: *n.* a group of alligators.

"If people want to find a native **congregation** of alligators, they'd do well to go to China or the United States, especially Louisiana or Florida."

COTERIE (KOH-tuh-ree): *n.* a group of prairie dogs.
"The stout-bodied rodents we saw in Mexico were a **coterie** of prairie dogs."

COWARDICE: *n.* a group of curs (aggressive dogs, especially mongrels).
"We were frightened by the **cowardice** of curs in the alley."

CRASH: *n.* a group of rhinos, which can also come in *stubbornnesses*.
"It is wise to move out of the way of a **crash** of charging rhinos."

CROSSING: *n.* a group of zebras, which can also come in *zeals*, *cohorts*, and *herds*.
"If you ever run into a **crossing** of zebras, you'll notice their high-pitched barking and whinnying."

CRY: *n.* a group of bloodhounds, which can also come in *sutes*.
"The fugitives tried to outrun the **cry** of bloodhounds."

GENERATION: *n.* a group of vipers, which can also come in *nests*.
"Denise was shaken up soon after her dream in which she was attacked by a **generation** of vipers."

GULP: *n.* a group of cormorants.
"Japanese and Chinese men would train a **gulp** of cormorants to catch fish for them by tying snares near the

bottoms of the birds' throats, allowing the birds to swallow only small fish and trapping larger fish, which the fishermen would remove from their mouths."

HUSK: *n.* a group of jackrabbits, which can also come in *droves* and *downs*.

"Although many jackrabbits are shy, one can sometimes see a **husk** of jackrabbits, especially in the spring, when there is competition among males to attain dominance and hence more access to breeding females."

IMPLAUSIBILITY: *n.* a group of gnus.

"When an **implausibility** migrates to new pastures, many of the gnus can be eaten by crocodiles living in rivers."

KETTLE: *n.* a group of vultures circling in rising currents of hot air (thermals), which can also come in *boils*.

"When vultures circle on thermals of hot air, they are said to resemble the rising bubbles in a boiling pot of water and are therefore called **kettles**."

LEAP: *n.* a group of leopards.

"We almost confused the **leap** of leopards with a group of cheetahs until we were told that leopards are larger and much more muscular than cheetahs."

LOUNGE: *n.* a group of lizards.

"The biologist assured us that the **lounge** of lizards we saw could pose no serious threats to human beings."

MISCHIEF: *n.* a group of mice.

"The family bought two cats to take care of the **mischief** of mice in the basement."

NIDE: *n.* a group of pheasants.

"When we saw the **nide** of pheasants, we noticed that the males were larger than the females and had longer tails."

OSTENTATION: *n.* a group of peacocks, which can also come in *musters* and *prides*.

"We saw an **ostentation** of peacocks with iridescent blue-green plumage, which turned out to be Indian peafowls."

PANDEMONIUM: *n.* from Milton's *Paradise Lost*, from Greek *pas*, *pantos* (all, the whole) and *daimon* (demon): a group of parrots, which also come in *companies*.

"In the 1770s, the explorer Captain Cook saw a **pandemonium** of Red Shining parrots in Tonga, an archipelago in the South Pacific."

PARLIAMENT: *n.* a group of owls.

"Because owls are mostly solitary, it is uncommon to see a **parliament** of owls in the wild."

PRICKLE: *n.* a group of porcupines.

"We saw a **prickle** of porcupines gnawing on car tires that we covered in rock salt."

QUIVER (KWIV-uhr): *n.* a group of cobras.

"When we saw hooded snakes in Egypt spitting their venom, we quickly realized that we had happened upon a **quiver** of cobras."

RAFTER: *n.* a group of turkeys.

"When I visited the farm, I had a headache and so was displeased by a **rafter** of gobbling turkeys."

RAG: *n.* a group of colts, which can also come in *rakes.*

"On the ranch, Bobby got to see a **rag** of two-year-old colts, some of which he rode."

RHUMBA: *n.* a group of rattlesnakes.

"The **rhumba** of rattlesnakes killed the mice in less than thirty seconds."

RICHNESS: *n.* a group of martens.

"Although martens, related to minks and weasels, are usually solitary, one can encounter a **richness** of them in late spring and early summer, as they meet to breed."

SCOURGE: *n.* a group of mosquitoes, properly named because they are responsible for more human deaths than any other creature.

"The **scourge** of mosquitoes preferred blond children to brunet adults."

SHREWDNESS: *n.* a group of apes.

"The **shrewdness** we encountered consisted of gibbons."

SKEIN (SKAYN): *n.* a group of geese *in flight* as opposed to on land or in water (a gaggle).

"We saw overhead a **skein** of Canada geese."

SKULK: *n.* a group of foxes, which can also come in *leashes*, *earths*, *leads*, and *troops.*

"The Australian shepherd was distressed by a **skulk** of foxes."

SLEUTH: *n.* a group of bears, which can also come in *sloths.*

"When we saw the **sleuth** of bears in the preserve, our

guide told us that a bear's sense of smell is in fact better than that of dogs."

SMACK: *n.* a group of jellyfish, which can also come in *broods* and *swarms*.

"A **smack** of jellyfish can not only sting people but also destroy fish nets, consume fish eggs, and even clog the engines of ships."

SORD: *n.* a group of mallards.

"In a **sord** of mallards, the breeding male stands out with his green head, black rear, and yellowish orange bill tipped with black (as opposed to the dark brown bill in females)."

Animals / Insects

BARROW: *n.* a male pig castrated before it reaches maturity.

"Meat from uncastrated adult pigs isn't as tasty to most people as meat from **barrows**."

BEEFALO: *n.* a hybrid animal that is five-eighths domestic cow and three-eighths American bison.

"Technically, a **beefalo** is more cow than bison."

BEESTINGS: *n.* the first milk given by a cow (or goat) after giving birth.

"A cow's **beestings** are particularly rich in nutrients."

BOAR: *n.* a male bear.

"Yogi Bear was the most famous **boar** in Jellystone Park."

BOOMER: *n.* a male kangaroo, which can be a *buck*, a *jack*, or sometimes even an *old man*.

"We saw a **boomer** red kangaroo that was six feet seven inches tall and weighed about two hundred pounds."

BROCKLEFACE: *n.* an animal having blotches of colored hair on an otherwise white face.

"Our dog was a **brockleface** with brown blotches on a predominately white face."

BUFORD: *n.* in rodeo performance, an animal that is easy to ride, rope, or throw down.

"In the rodeo, Duke was happy to get a **buford** in the steer-roping event."

CAMA: *n.* a hybrid animal produced from a camel and a llama.

"Because a dromedary camel is about six times heavier than a llama, creating a hybrid—a **cama**—requires artificial insemination."

CARUNCLES: *n. pl.* from Latin *caruncula* (little pieces of flesh): the fleshy bulbous bumps found on the neck and heads of turkeys.

"When we looked at the necks of the turkeys, we noticed that the **caruncles** on the male turkeys (*gob-*

blers or *toms*) were larger than those on female turkeys (*hens*)."

CHELA (KEE-luh): *n.* the large claw of a lobster or a crab.
  "He enjoyed eating a lobster's **chela**."

COB: *n.* a male swan.
  "Unlike male human beings, **cobs** are truly monogamous, forming bonds with female swans (*see* PEN) that last for many years and sometimes for life."

COBBY: *adj.* especially of cats, dogs, and horses, stocky—that is, short and compact in proportion.
  "Because of their broad and round bodies, broad feet, and short legs, Persian and exotic shorthairs are said to be **cobby** felines."

COUCHANT (KOW-chuhnt): *adj.* from Old French *couchier* (to lie down): in heraldry, an animal lying down with the head up.
  "On the shield, we saw a lion **couchant**, relaxing but awake."

COW: *n.* a female dinosaur.
  "The scientist asserted that evidence suggests that among the tyrannosaurus rex, **cows** had larger hips than the males."

COYDOG (KY-dawg): *n.* a hybrid animal produced by a male coyote and female feral dog found in parts of the northeastern United States.
  "Because coyotes tend to be solitary by nature and **coydogs** tend to be unsociable, **coydogs** are usually unsuitable as pets."

CRIA (CREE-ah): *n.* a baby llama, alpaca, vicuna, and other related animals.

"If you have a llama that has recently given birth, it is wise to shear her so that a **cria** can more easily find the right place to nurse and avoid ingesting fiber, which can kill it."

CROCHE (KROHSH): *n.* from Middle French *croche* (hook): a small knob on the antlers of deer and some other antlered animals.

"The child wanted to touch the **croche** about the top of the deer's antler."

CROCKLET: *n.* a baby crocodile.

"Even though a **crocklet** may not have the bite force of an adult crocodile (whose bite force is more than ten times that of a great white shark), you would be unwise to stick your hand near a **crocklet's** open jaws."

DEAD SET: *n.* a hunting dog's stance when pointing to prey.

"When the dog was in a **dead set**, his eyes were focused on his prey in undivided attention."

DEWLAP: *n.* (i) a loose, hanging fold of skin under the neck of a cow or an ox; (ii) a corresponding fold of skin on other animals, including dogs (such as the basset hound and mastiff) and geese.

"When we looked at the Neapolitan mastiff's neck, we saw a large **dewlap** on a huge dog."

DOBBIN (DAHB-uhn): *n.* from *Dobbin*, alteration of *Robin*, nickname for *Robert*: a horse, especially, a working farm horse.

"Amos asked Luke to hitch the plow to the **dobbin**."

DOE: *n.* a female mouse.

"Pixie was the male mouse, and Dixie was the **doe**."

DRAKE: *n.* a male duck.

"Donald Duck could properly be called Donald **Drake** because he is male."

EPIZOOTIC (EP-i-zoh-**AHT**-ik): *n.* of animals, unexpectedly widespread among animals of a single kind within a particular region.

"In 1990, Newcastle disease virus was **epizootic** in double-crested cormorant colonies on the Great Lakes, killing about ten thousand birds."

FLEWS: *n.* the overhanging lateral parts of the upper lips of dogs, especially hounds.

"Because of their large **flews**, bloodhounds can fling saliva about twenty feet with one shake of their heads."

FLYER: *n.* a female kangaroo, which can also be called a *doe* or *jill.*

"Because of her pouch, we knew that we were looking at a **flyer** and not a male kangaroo."

FREEMARTIN: *n.* an infertile female mammal that has masculine behavior and nonfunctioning ovaries.

"The female calf was a **freemartin**, having been sterilized in the womb by hormones from a male twin."

GEE: *v. imp.* to command to animals, such as horses and oxen, to turn right.

"When the equestrian shouted, '**Gee!**,' the horse turned to the right."

GIB (GIB): *n.* a castrated male ferret (*see* HOB), as well as a castrated male cat.

"The vet said that turning my male ferret into a **gib** was a simple and safe procedure that would not only prevent him from impregnating females (*see* JILL) but also blunt aggressive tendencies, making him less likely to fight."

GILT: *n.* a young female pig that hasn't given birth.

"When a **gilt** produces a litter of piglets, she becomes a sow."

GINGERING: *n.* the practice of inserting ginger into a horse's anus to make the horse more lively or to make it carry its tail high.

"**Gingering** (which used to be called *feaguing*) is now generally forbidden in horse shows, though the practice has in the past been used especially in Arabian and American saddlebred breeds, where animation and high tail carriage are much desired."

GRUNTLE: *n.* a pig's snout.

"The **gruntle** on a miniature potbellied pig is longer than that of a domestic pig, though both animals have a keen sense of smell."

GUARDANT (GAHR-duhnt): *adj.* in heraldry, having the head toward the spectator—said of a heraldic animal whose head is turned at ninety degrees from the rest of the body.

"On the shield, we saw a lion **guardant**."

HAW: *v. imp.* to command animals, such as horses and oxen, to turn left.

"When the farmer shouted, 'Haw!,' the ox turned to the left."

HIBERNACULUM: *n.* a shelter in which an animal or a dormant insect resides during dormancy or hibernation.

"The bear's **hibernaculum** was a cave."

HINNY: *n.* from Latin *hinnus* (mule): the hybrid off-spring of a male horse and a female donkey.

"**Hinnies** are on average slightly smaller than mules, and their heads resemble the heads of horses more than the heads of donkeys."

HOB: *n.* a male ferret.

"We figured that the largest ferret in front of us was a **hob** and not a female."

JILL: *n.* a female ferret.

"Although an unfixed ferret is nearly always cheaper than a fixed one, we wanted to buy a fixed **jill**."

JOEY: *n.* a baby kangaroo.

"When a **joey** is born, it is tiny compared to an adult kangaroo—about the size of a lima bean."

KHEDA (KED-uh): *n.* in Myanmar and other parts of South Asia, an enclosure used to capture wild elephants.

"In India, we were surprised to see how cooperative the elephants were when they were driven into a **kheda**."

KITTEN: *n.* a baby mouse, which can also be called a *pinkie* or a *pup*.

"When Jeff told us that his niece was playing with a

kitten, we thought that he was talking about a young cat rather than a baby mouse."

KOOMKIE: *n.* a trained female elephant used to attract wild males.

"Sarah was wondering why male elephants were following her until she realized that she was riding a **koomkie**."

LEVERET (LEV-uhr-it): *n.* from Middle French *levre* (hare): a hare under one year of age.

"A newly born **leveret**, unlike a newly born rabbit, is born fully furred and with open eyes."

LORE: *n.* the region between the eye and bill on the side of a bird's head.

"Many species of birds have areas of colored skin on their faces, especially on the **lores**."

MACHO: *n.* a male llama.

"Although female llamas reach puberty in about one year, **machos** don't become sexually mature until about three years."

MEDUSA: *n.* from the mythological *Medusa*, a female monster (a Gorgon) with snakes for hair and the ability to turn people to stone with her glance: an adult jellyfish.

"By the time a jellyfish develops into a **medusa**, it has tentacles."

MONOTREME: *n.* from Greek *monos* (single) and *trema* (hole), indicating that the animals have only one bodily orifice (cloaca) for reproduction, urination, and defecation: an egg-laying mammal with one bodily orifice for reproduction, urination, and defecation.

"Although nearly all mammals bear live young, **monotremes**, such as the platypus and the echidna, lay eggs."

NASUTE (nay-SOOT): *n.* from Latin *nasutus* (big-nosed): a soldier termite with a beak-like snout through which a sticky secretion repellent to other insects is emitted.

"When looking under rocks in Gardner Canyon in Arizona's Santa Rita Mountains, we saw **nasutes** and noticed their pointy snouts, through which they spray attackers, especially ants."

PELAGE (PEL-ij): *n.* from Latin *pilus* (hair): the hairy covering of a mammal.

"The coloration of the chocolate Lab's **pelage** resembled that of the **pelage** of the brown dog of another breed."

PEN: *n.* a female swan.

"Although male and female swans have similar plumage, males are generally bigger and heavier than **pens**."

PIZZLE: *n.* from Middle Low German *pēse* (bowstring): a penis of an animal, especially a bull.

"When Zack, a seventh-grader, drew a bull with an erect **pizzle**, the teacher reprimanded him."

PLANTIGRADE: *adj.* from Latin *planta* (sole of the foot) and *-gradus* (going): walking with the entire sole of the foot on the ground, as human beings, bears, raccoons, rats, and many other animals do.

"Although cats, dogs, and most other animals walk on their digits or toes, human beings, bears, pandas, skunks, and some other animals use **plantigrade** locomotion."

POLLARD: *n.* from Middle English *pol* (top of the head, head): (i) an animal that is usually horned but has either shed its horns or had them removed; (ii) a tree cut back to the trunk to promote growth of a dense head of foliage.

"Because the only goats Michelle had seen had horns, she immediately noticed the **pollard**."

POMP: *n.* a group of Pekingese/Pekinese.

"When we saw the **pomp**, we immediately noticed the broad, flat faces of Pekingeses."

RANARIUM: *n.* a frog farm.

"The three-year-old girl was frightened by hearing dozens of frogs at the **ranarium**."

RANGY: *n.* of cats, long limbed and long bodied.

"The COBBY (*see*) cat and his **rangy** feline friend made a sharp contrast."

RETROMINGENT (RE-truh-MIN-juhnt): *adj.* from Latin *retro-* (backward, back, behind) and *mingere* (to urinate): urinating backward, as camels, hippos, hares, raccoons, and so on.

"When people watch camels wrestling, they are advised to keep their distance to avoid flying urine from those **retromingent** animals."

SOW: *n.* a female bear.

"The **sow** can be at least as protective of her cubs as a male bear."

TIGLON (TY-gluhn): *n.* a hybrid cross between a male tiger and a female lion (lioness).

"Producing **tiglons** is trickier than producing tigers or lions because male tigers often have trouble reading a lioness's behavioral cues in courtship."

TUMBLER: *n.* the pupa stage of a mosquito.

"Although adult mosquitoes can eat, **tumblers**, which breathe through tubes on their backs called siphons, cannot eat."

WAY-WISE: *adj.* of a horse, well broken, especially for use on the road or on a racetrack.

"The inexperienced rider needed a **way-wise** horse, not a refractory one."

WETHER (WETH-uhr): *n.* a castrated ram or billy goat.

"Uncastrated rams grow faster than **wethers**, though **wethers** are easier to manage and eliminate the possibilities of early or unwanted pregnancies."

ZEBRULA (ZEE-bruh-luh, ZEB-ruh-luh): *n.* the offspring of a male zebra and a female horse.

"Although **zebrulas** are good for transporting things, they have a wild side and shouldn't be ridden by novices."

ZONY: *n.* the offspring of a male zebra and a female pony.

"Although zebras have been crossed with smaller pony breeds such as the Shetland, medium-size pony mares are preferred when producing riding **zonies**."

Appliances

AGITATOR: *n.* the apparatus in the middle of a washing machine that stirs the clothes around.

"Because we had overloaded the clothes, the **agitator** was barely moving."

BIGGIN: *n.* from Mr. *Biggin*, inventor of a coffee percolator: the part of a coffeepot holding the grounds.

"Jerry's **biggin** didn't require liners for the coffee grounds."

CRUMBER: *n.* a miniature carpet sweeper for removing crumbs from a tablecloth, tabletop, or lap.

"The server used a **crumber** to remove some bread crumbs from our table."

GLASS ENVELOPE: *n.* the thin layer of glass surrounding the light bulb mechanism and the inert gases.

"The **glass envelope** of a light bulb is supposed to keep out oxygen."

GUILLEMETS (GIL-uh-mets): *n. pl.* also called *angle quotes*, line segments appearing as pairs of pointed arrows (« »), used as quotation marks in French and as symbols on electronic devices for *rewind* or *fast forward* (« »).

"We noticed the **guillemets** on the Walkman."

REAMER: *n.* the twirling part of a juicing machine that removes the pulp and juice.

"The **reamer** on our juicer was so powerful that it thoroughly removed the pulp from any fruit."

TOAST WELL: *n.* the name of the slot in a toaster in which bread is placed.

"We recommended to Jerry that he unplug the toaster before sticking a knife into the **toast well** to retrieve a slice of bread."

ARCHITECTURE

CAFETORIUM: *n.* a large room common in industrial and military installation that combines the function of a cafeteria and an auditorium.

"The colonel briefed his men in the **cafetorium** after lunch."

CAMPANILE (KAM-puh-NEE-lee): *n.* from Italian *campana* (bell): a bell tower, especially a freestanding one (in American usage).

"The tallest **campanile** in the world, as of 2010, is the Joseph Chamberlain Memorial Clock Tower at the University of Birmingham in England, the bells of which weigh twenty tons and are housed in a tower whose height exceeds the length of an American football field."

CAPITAL: *n.* from Latin *caput* (head): in architecture, the crowning member of a column.

"The **capital** of a column sits on the shaft, which in turn sits on the base."

CHANCEL: *n.* from Latin *cancelli* (lattice): the part of a church around the altar at the east end of a traditional Christian church.

"The **chancel** usually contains not only the altar but also seats for the ministers and, in Anglican and Methodist churches, will usually include the choir."

CRENEL (KREN-uhl): *n.* the cut-off portion or space in defensive architecture atop walls or castles used for discharging arrows or other missiles.

"Also known as *camels*, *embrasures*, *loops*, or *wheelers*, **crenels** were next to solid parts of a parapet (*see* MERLON) to enable soldiers to gain cover from arrows and other missiles."

CROTCH: *n.* in handball, racquetball, and squash, the intersection of two surfaces, such as the front wall and the floor.

"In racquetball, a shot hitting the **crotch** results in side-out or a point."

GRIMTHORPE (GRIM-thorp): *v.* from first Baron *Grimthorpe*, who was an English lawyer and architect who lived principally in the nineteenth century and who was severely criticized for the way in which he tried to restore St. Albans Cathedral in England: to remodel (an ancient building) without proper knowledge or care to retain its original quality and character.

"It was a mistake to let an inexperienced architect **grimthorpe** the historic building."

HYPAETHRAL (hy-PEE-thruhl): *adj.* from Latin *hypaethrus* (in the open air), from Greek *hypaithros*, from *hypo-*, *hupo* (under), and *aithēr* (ether, air, sky): wholly or partly open to the sky.

"In the movie *High Anxiety*, Dr. Richard H. Thorndyke (Mel Brooks) has a scene in which birds are profusely defecating on him, leading him to run into a building that he didn't realize was **hypaethral**."

MACHICOLATION (muh-CHIK-uh-LAY-shuhn): *n.* from Latin *maccare* (to crush) and *collum* (neck): a floor opening, parapet, or other place from which hot lead, boiling water, rocks, and other objects can be dropped on an enemy.

"**Machicolations** were often used to defend medieval castles from invaders."

MAQUETTE (ma-KET): *n.* from Latin *macula* (spot): a usually small model of a room or a sculpture to gauge its appearance or composition.

"The **maquette** helped us predict what the room would look like when it was completed."

MERLON (MUHR-luhn): *n.* any of the solid intervals between spaces (*see* CRENEL) in a battlement surmounting a wall, as in a castle or other fortified building.

"**Merlons** in Roman times were wide enough to shelter a single man but were enlarged in the Middle Ages and provided with loopholes for which crossbows were sometimes used."

MIHRAB (MEE-ruhb): *n.* a niche or chamber in a mosque indicating the direction of Mecca and usually containing a copy of the Qur'an.

"Because Muslims are required to worship facing Mecca, a **mihrab** enables them to face in that direction in any mosque."

MINARET: a slender tower of a mosque, containing a balcony from which a crier (muezzin) calls Muslims to prayer.

"Every day the muezzin calls Muslims to prayer from a **minaret**."

NAVE: *n.* from Greek *naus* (ship): the long, narrow central walkway in a cruciform (cross-shaped) church that rises higher than the aisles flanking it.

"Technically, a bride doesn't walk down an aisle, which is on each side of a church, but the **nave**."

TRANSEPT: *n.* from Latin *trans-*, *tra-* (across, to the other side) and *septum*, *saeptum* (enclosure, wall): the area that crosses the central vertical walkway (*see* NAVE) of a church, separating that walkway from the sanctuary.

"To get to the altar, we walked down the NAVE (*see*) and walked across the **transept**."

VOMITORIUM (VAHM-uh-**TOR**-ee-uhm): *n.* a large opening that serves as a passageway for people entering and leaving athletic stadiums.

"We didn't leave until most of the baseball fans had walked through the **vomitorium**."

VOUSSOIR (voo-SWAHR): *n.* from Latin *volvere* (to turn, roll): one of the wedge-shaped stones forming the curved parts of an arch or vaulted ceiling.

"The top **voussoir** of an arch is called the *keystone*."

Arrangements /
Positions

ANTEPENULTIMATE: *n.* from Late Latin *antepaenultima*, feminine of *antepaenultimus* (preceding the next to last): third to last.

"The **antepenultimate** letter of our alphabet is *x*."

COFFLE (KAHF-uhl): *n.* from Arabic *qāfila* (caravan): a line of convicts, slaves, or animals fastened together.

"Woody Allen once played a convict in a **coffle** in the movie *Take the Money and Run*."

FROG-MARCH: *v.* to carry (as a resisting prisoner) face-down by the arms and legs.

"When the prisoner refused to walk, the guards decided to **frog-march** him."

QUINCUNX (KWIN-kuhnks): *n.* from Latin *quincunx* (five-twelfths): an arrangement of things by five in a square, as in the pips on a die (:·:).

"The bushes were planted in a **quincunx**."

Art / Photography

CRAQUELURE (krak-LOOR): *n.* from French *craqueler* (to crack): a network of hairline cracks common to old oil paintings.

"The **craquelure** in the *Mona Lisa*, as in other old art, can make the art difficult to forge because it is difficult to duplicate the fine patterns of cracks."

DAUB: *n.* a poorly painted picture.

"Although the abstract expressionist paintings of Jackson Pollock fetch a huge price nowadays, many people during his day considered his paintings **daubs**."

MAULSTICK: *n.* from the Dutch *maalstok* (painter's stick): a stick with a soft leather or padded head used by painters to rest a hand while working.

"In numerous paintings from the sixteenth through the nineteenth centuries, **maulsticks** are often included as part of the artist's equipment, at times showing artists resting their hands on them."

OPUSCULE (**OH**-puhs-SKYOOL): *n.* a small or petty work.

"The composer had neither the time nor the talent to produce a great work, but he could quickly produce **opuscules**."

PUTTO (POO-toh, POOT-toh): *n.* from Italian *putto* (boy): in art, a figure of a young boy (as a cupid) often found in decorative painting and sculpture, especially of the Renaissance or Baroque periods.

"The **putto** was depicted as naked and winged."

STIPPLE: *v.* in painting, to apply small dots of the same color of paint to produce an even or softly graded shadow.

"The nature of the shade in the painting revealed that the painting had been **stippled**."

Astronomy

APHELION (uh-FEE-lee-uhn, uh-FEEL-yuhn): *n.* from New Latin *aphelium*, from Greek *apo-* (apart) and *hēlios* (sun): the point in the orbit of a heavenly body that is farthest from the sun.

"During Neptune's aphelion, it is farther from the sun than Pluto is."

ASTROBLEME (AS-truh-BLEEM): *n.* from Greek *astro-*, *astron* (star) and *blēma* (missile, wound from a missile): a usually circular scar on the Earth's surface left from the impact of a meteorite.

"We saw our first **astrobleme** when we visited the Barringer Crater in Arizona."

ASTRONOMICAL UNIT: *n.* a unit of length equal to about 149,597,871 kilometers or 92,955,807 miles, representing the mean distance between the Earth and the sun over one Earth orbit.

"Pluto is 39.5 **astronomical units** from the sun."

GIBBOUS (GIB-uhs, JIB-uhs): *n.* from Middle English *gibbous* (bulging), from Late Latin *gibbosus* (hunch-backed), from Latin *gibbus* (hump): of the Moon or a planet, more than half but less than fully illuminated.

"From the Northern Hemisphere, people can see 51 to 99 percent of the right half of the Moon during its waxing **gibbous** phase."

MARE: *n.* from Latin *mare* (sea): one of the several dark areas on the surface of either the Moon or Mars, originally thought to be seas.

"Perhaps the best-known **mare** on the Moon is the Sea of Tranquility, which has a diameter of 873 kilometers and which contains a basin of basalt."

MOONBOW: *n.* a phenomenon resembling a rainbow, produced by light reflected off the surface of the Moon rather than direct sunlight.

"**Moonbows**, which are somewhat faint, are always in the part of the sky opposite from that of the Moon."

BIOLOGY

ALTRICIAL (al-TRISH-uhl): *n.* from Latin *alere* (to nourish): in biology, helpless, immobile, without hair or down, and often blind at birth or hatching.

"Herons and owls are **altricial**, whereas ground-nesting birds such as ducks or turkeys are able to leave the nest in one or two days."

AMPLEXUS (am-PLEK-suhs): *n.* from Latin *amplexus* (an embracing): the mating embrace of frogs and toads during which the male fertilizes the female's eggs.

"The sixth-graders giggled when they saw the **amplexus** of the mating frogs in the woods."

CLEPTOBIOSIS (KLEP-toh-by-OH-sis): *n.* from Greek *klepto-* (theft), from *kleptein* (to steal) and *-biosis* (mode of life): the act of plundering food, as when members of one species steal food from another species.

"Although ants are known for their organization and productivity, ants of some species will engage in **cleptobiosis** for food."

CRESPUSCULAR (kre-PUHS-kyuh-luhr): *adj.* from Latin *crepusculum* (dusk, twilight): (i) of, relating to, or like twilight; (ii) active in the twilight (dawn and dusk).

"**Crespuscular** creatures, such as moose, rabbits, ferrets, guinea pigs, hamsters, and skunks, can minimize contact with those predators that either forage most intensely at night or are most active at midday."

DIURNATION (DY-uhr-**NAY**-shuhn): *n.* from Latin *diurnus* (of the day, daily) and English *-ation*: the habit of sleeping or becoming dormant by day.

"Unlike most people, who are awake and active during daylight, bats are known for **diurnation**."

DUFF: *n.* the partly decayed organic matter on the forest floor.

"The **duff** we saw consisted of leaves, branches, bark, and stems in various stages of decomposition."

ESTIVATE (ES-tuh-vayt): *v.* from Latin *aestivatus*, past participle of *aestivare* (to reside during the summer): to pass the summer in a dormant state.

"Sheila was a public-school teacher who loved to **estivate** three months."

EUTOCIA (yoo-TOH-shee-uh): *n.* from Greek *eutokia*, from *eutokos* (giving birth easily): normal childbirth.

"Because not every childbirth is a **eutocia**, it is important for people to prepare for complications."

FRASS: *n.* insect excrement.

"We noticed some more **frass** on the floor and decided to call the exterminator."

GOSSAMER: *n.* a fine film of cobwebs often seen floating in the air or caught on bushes or grass.

"The film we saw on the bushes looked like silk but was actually **gossamer**, produced by some spiders."

LENTIC (LEN-tik): *adj.* from Latin *lentus* (slow, calm, sluggish): of, relating to, or living in still waters (as lakes, ponds, and swamps).

"For meditation, I prefer the **lentic** calm of a lake to the roar of the ocean."

LIMICOLOUS (ly-MIK-uh-luhs): *adj.* from Latin *limus* (mud, slime) and *-colous* (dwelling): living in mud.

"The long, slender **limicolous** creature was an earthworm."

LOTIC (LOHD-ik, LOH-tik): *adj.* from Latin *lotus* (action of washing or bathing), from *lautus*, *lotus*, past participle of *lavere* (to wash): of, relating to, or living in actively moving water (as in stream currents or waves).

"Jessie felt calm when she heard the **lotic** sounds near her beachfront home."

LUCIFERIN: *n.* from *lucifer* (light bringing): light-emitting biological pigment found in certain organisms, such as fireflies.

"Fireflies contain **luciferin**, which helps them produce and emit light."

MERDIVOROUS (mur-DIV-ur-us): *adj.* from Latin *merda* (excrement) and English suffix *-vorous* (eating): feeding on excrement.

"The scarab is a **merdivorous** beetle."

MULM: *n.* the organic sediment (sludge) that collects at the bottom of an aquarium, consisting of fish excrement, decaying plant matter, and other dreck.

"In an aquarium containing plants, **mulm** is slowly digested over the months by the bacteria living there and is broken into useful chemicals that plants and other life living in the gravel can absorb."

NIDIFICATE (NID-i-fi-kayt): *v.* from Latin *nidificatus*, past participle of *nidificare* (to build a nest): to build a nest.

"Birds **nidificate** by instinct, not by training."

NULLIPARA (nuh-LIP-uh-ruh): *n.* from Latin *nullus* (not, none, no) and *parere* (to produce, bring forth): a childless woman.

"After five years of marriage, Dawn, who had been a **nullipara**, had a baby."

OCELLUS (oh-SEL-uhs): *n.* from Latin *ocellus* (little eye), diminutive of *oculus* (eye): an eye-like colored spot on animals or plants, as on peacock feathers or butterfly wings, or on a leaf of a plant.

"The **ocelli** on peacock feathers have fascinated people because of how the spots resemble eyes."

PESSIMAL: *adj.* of an organism's environment, least favorable for survival.

"Putting a plant that requires a good deal of sunlight into a dark closet is putting it into a **pessimal** environment."

PRIMIPARA (pry-MIP-uhr-uh): *n.* from New Latin *primipara* (individual having only one child): a woman who is pregnant for the first time, or a woman who has given birth to only one child.

"The woman with five kids turned to the **primipara** who was about to give birth and said, 'I can help you with your newborn because I have lots of experience.'"

SAPROPHAGOUS (sa-PRAHF-uh-gus): *adj.* from Greek *sapr-, sapros* (rotten) and *-phagus, phagein* (to eat): feeding on dead or decaying animal matter.

"The carcass of the bird was covered with **saprophagous** insects."

TRAVAIL: *n.* childbirth pangs.

"Some Presbyterians in Scotland argued against the use of chloroform during childbirth on the grounds that the Bible in Genesis says that women shall experience **travail**."

~~~~~~

BOATING

~~~~~~

BITT: *n.* a short thick post on the deck of a ship for securing ropes or cables.

"The sailors were instructed to tie the ropes to a **bitt**."

BOLLARD: *n.* the dock post to which a boat is tied.

"Because the boat wasn't securely tied to the **bollard**, it began to float away from the dock."

BOWER ANCHOR: *n.* the main or largest anchor on a ship.

"The **bower anchor** is carried in the bow of a ship."

BREAM: *v.* to clean (a ship's bottom) by fire and scraping.

"The ship's bottom had to be **breamed** to remove barnacles and debris."

BURGEE (buhr-JEE): *n.* a triangular identifying flag of a yacht club flown on boats by members.

"Although **burgees** may be flown day or night, they aren't flown in races, which instead call for a square racing flag."

CALF: *n.* a small mass of floating ice, separated from a glacier or iceberg.

"We couldn't determine what the floating object was until we got close to it, when we discovered that it was a **calf** detached from a floe."

CAPESIZE: *adj.* being too large to navigate the Suez Canal to and from the Arabian Gulf.

"A **capesize** vessel, because it is too large to navigate the Suez Canal, is forced to voyage around the Cape of Good Hope or Cape Horn when it must travel between oceans."

CAT'S-PAW: *n.* a slight breeze that ruffles the surface of the sea in irregular patches during a calm.

"The sailor, when gazing at the water, noticed a **cat's-paw**, making him feel even more relaxed."

COMPANIONWAY: *n.* a ship's stairway running from one deck to another.

"To get to the deck above us, I climbed a **companionway**."

DAVIT (DAY-vuht): *n.* a ship's crane used for holding or hoisting ship's boats, anchors, or cargo.

"The **davit** held the lifeboat in place."

DUNNAGE (DUHN-ij): *n.* mats, pieces of wood, or other loose material placed under or among cargo in the hold of a ship to keep the cargo dry and protect it from damage.

"The sailors used blankets and mats as **dunnage** to protect their fragile cargo."

ESKIMO ROLL: in kayaking, a complete rollover, in which the kayak goes into and under the water and back up.

"Although Peter was not harmed by the **Eskimo roll**, he did inhale some water when the kayak rolled over."

LAGAN (LAG-uhn): *n.* goods thrown into the sea with a buoy attached so that they can be found again.

"Because of the buoys we saw attached to the floating nets, we knew that we had come upon **lagan** rather than flotsam."

PIROGUE (PEE-rohg, PI-rohg, PUH-rohg): *n.* a canoe produced from a hollow trunk of a single tree.

"The natives on the island created **pirogues** from local trees."

SHANK: *n.* the vertical stem of an anchor.

"The **shank** is the longest part of the anchor."

SPOONDRIFT: *n.* a spray blown from waves during a gale at sea.

"Because of the gale when we were sailing, we got wet from the **spoondrift**."

TAFFRAIL (TAF-rayl, TAF-ruhl): *n.* (i) the rail around the stern of a ship; (ii) the flat upper part of the stern of a vessel, made of wood and often ornately carved.

"We held to the **taffrail** as we looked at the water from the stern of the vessel."

THALASSOCRACY (THAL-uh-**SAHK**-ruh-see): *n.* from Greek *thalassokratia*, from *thalassa* (sea) and *-kratia* (rule): maritime supremacy.

"The British navy once enjoyed **thalassocracy**."

THWART: *n.* a rower's seat extending across a boat.

"We sat on the **thwart** as we rowed the boat."

YAW: *v.* to swerve off course momentarily or temporarily, as when a boat or plane deviates along the vertical axis.

"The boat **yawed** because of a heavy wave."

Bodily Products / Effects / Functions

BORBORYGMUS (BOHR-buh-**RIG**-muhs): *n.* from Greek *borboryzein* (to rumble): a rumbling noise made by the movement of fluids and gas (including food, acids, and digestive juices) from the stomach into the upper part of the small intestine.

"The refined woman was embarrassed by her **borborygmus** after dinner."

BROMIDROSIS (BROH-mi-**DROH**-sis): *n.* the secretion of foul-smelling sweat.

"The man's **bromidrosis** was so potent during his workout that the gym manager sprayed a room deodorant around him."

CERUMEN (suh-**ROO**-muhn): *n.* from Latin *cera* (wax): earwax.

"When removing **cerumen** from your ear with a cotton swab rather than with a solution, you need to be careful to avoid injury."

CHLOASMA (**KLOH**-az-muh): *n.* from Greek *chloazein* (to be green): a skin discoloration marked by yellowish brown pigmented patches or spots: "liver spots."

"Because of hormonal changes, **chloasma** is common on the skin of pregnant women and women taking oral or patch contraceptives or hormone replacement therapy."

CREPITUS: *n.* a crackling sound heard in the chest of someone with a lung disease such as pneumonia.

"We heard a **crepitus** as the man with the pneumonia was breathing."

PILOERECTION (py-**LOH**-i-**REK**-shuhn): *n.* from Latin *pilus* (hair) and English *erection*: erection of hair on the skin, as in goose bumps.

"**Piloerection** occurs when a stimulus such as cold or fright causes a discharge from the involuntary nervous system, triggering the contraction of little muscles."

SINGULTUS (sing-**GUHL**-tuhs): *n.* from Latin *singultus* (hiccup, sob, cluck): a hiccup.

"When the dainty woman released a **singultus**, she was

relieved that no embarrassing sound came out of her other end."

~~~~~~~~~~~~~~~~~~~~~~~~

Books

~~~~~~~~~~~~~~~~~~~~~~~~

BESTIARY: *n.* a book with illustrations of animals accompanied by moral lessons.

"According to many **bestiaries**, the pelican, which was believed to tear open its breast to give birth, is a living representation of Jesus."

BIBLIOCLAST (BIB-lee-OH-klast): *n.* from Greek *biblio-*, *biblion* (book) and Greek *-clast*, *klan* (to break): one who mutilates or destroys books.

"In Nazi Germany, as in other totalitarian regimes, **biblioclasts** have destroyed books hostile to the rulers."

BIBLIOKLEPT (BIB-lee-uh-klept): *n.* from Greek *biblio-* (book) and *kleptein* (to steal): one who steals books.

"In recent decades, **biblioklepts** have especially liked to steal *The Joy of Sex* and its sequels."

BIBLIOPOLE (BIB-lee-uh-POHL): *n.* from Latin *bibliopola*, from Greek *bibliopōlēs*, from *biblio-*, *biblios* (paper, book scroll) and *pōlein* (to sell, barter): a dealer in books, especially used or rare ones.

"The **bibliopole** prided himself on having obscure books, including those on sperm motility."

CARD PLATE: *n.* in book publishing, the book page containing a list of books by the same author.

"Because Isaac Asimov wrote hundreds of books, his **card plates** didn't list most of his books."

FOREL (FOR-uhl): *n.* from Middle English *forel* (case, sheath): a sheath or open-ended box for holding a book.

"The book of Aristotle's complete works was sold in a **forel**, which protected it."

GRANGERIZE (GRAYN-juh-RYZ): *v.* from James *Granger* (a nineteenth-century English biographer): (i) to mutilate (a book or periodical) to obtain material for one's own book; (ii) to extra-illustrate, that is, to illustrate a book with pictures taken from published sources, such as by clipping them out for one's own use.

"The elderly man would go to stores and libraries to **grangerize** pictures of glamorous actresses."

SLUSH PILE: *n.* stacks of unsolicited typescripts that pile up at publishing houses.

"An unsolicited and unagented typescript from a first-time author with no credentials is very likely to end up in a **slush pile**."

THUMB INDEXES: *n. pl.* the indentations on the side of a dictionary.

Because I have access to unabridged dictionaries over the Internet, I rarely touch the **thumb indexes** of dictionaries."

Botany

PHLOEM BUNDLES (FLOH-em): *n.* stringy bits between the skin and the edible parts of a banana involved in transporting nutrients.

"The **phloem bundles** on a banana are part of its vascular system, carrying nutrients to various parts of the fruit."

PLUMCOT: *n.* a hybrid between a plum and an apricot.

"A **plumcot**, which has a smooth skin, is more plum-like than apricot-like."

RAMPIKE: *n.* a standing dead tree or tree stump, especially one killed by fire.

"We were saddened to see that, after the forest fire, many old trees had become **rampikes**."

RUDERAL (ROO-duhr-uhl): *adj.* from New Latin *ruderalis*, from Late Latin *rudus*, *ruder-* (rubbish, rubble): of plants, growing in rubbish, poor land, or waste.

"We found a few **ruderal** plants in the junkyard."

SUGAR SPOT: *n.* a brown speck appearing on banana skins.

"The little girl saw the **sugar spots** on the banana and called them freckles."

WATER-SICK: *adj.* unproductive because of excessive irrigation.

"He was told that he wouldn't be able to grow vegetables in the **water-sick** soil."

~~~~~~

BROADCASTING

~~~~~~

LAVALIERE (LAV-uh-LEER): *n.* a microphone worn around the neck, as a necklace.

"The TV talk show host preferred a **lavaliere** to a microphone she would have to carry in her hand."

QUONKING: *n.* background noise (as from conversation) that disturbs or disrupts a TV or radio show; also known as *mike stew*.

"The meteorologist's fart was embarrassing **quonking** that gave viewers a good laugh."

Building /
Construction

ASHLAR (ASH-luhr): *n.* stone that is evenly cut and carefully laid, as distinguished from masonry using rough, odd-shaped stones ("rubble masonry").

"**Ashlar** blocks are large and rectangular and usually thirteen to fifteen inches in height; when smaller than eleven inches, they are usually known as small **ashlar**."

FROG: *n.* in construction, the hollow holding mortar in the top of a building brick.

"The builder needed to clear the **frog** of debris before adding the mortar."

HA-HA: *n.* a fence or wall set in a ditch around a garden or park so as not to hide the view from within.

"**Ha-has** are still found in the grounds of grand country houses and estates, where they keep the cattle and sheep in the pastures and out of the formal gardens without an obtrusive fence."

MORTISE (MOR-tuhs): *n.* a hole or slot cut into a piece of wood, stone, or other material for a projecting part (*see* TENON) to form a joint.

"The carpenter was happy that the **mortise** was exactly one inch deep."

PALISADE: *n.* a fence of wooden stakes used as a defensive barrier.

"Although **palisades** were easily built from materials readily available and were effective for short-term conflicts against small forces, they were vulnerable to fire."

SKINTLE: *v.* to set (bricks) irregularly to give a quaint or picturesque affect.

"After six-year-old Vanessa said that bricklayers were sloppy when they laid bricks for the house down the street, we pointed out that the bricks were **skintled** to achieve the unusual effect."

TENON (TEN-uhn): *n.* from Old French *tenir* (to hold): a projecting part cut on the end of a piece of wood or other material for insertion into a corresponding hole (*see* MORTISE) in another piece to make a joint.

"Because part of the **tenon** became chipped, it weakened the joint."

TESSERA (TESS-er-uh): *n.* from Greek *tesseres* (four), as in the four corners of a piece used to create a mosaic pattern: a small piece of stone, glass, or some other material used in making a mosaic pattern.

"A **tessera** is to a mosaic as a paver is to a patio."

TOENAILING: *v.* to drive a nail at such an angle that it penetrates a second piece of wood.

"The carpenter drove the nail in at an angle, **toenailing** the stud to the plate."

Clocks

GNOMON (NOH-muhn): *n.* from Greek *gnōmōn* (interpreter, discerner, pointer on a sundial, carpenter's square): the triangular part of a sundial that casts a shadow indicating the time.

"A sundial without a **gnomon** is about as useful as an analog watch without its hands."

Clothing

AGLET (AG-lit): *n.* from Middle French *aguillette* (small needle): a metal or plastic tube fixed around each end of a shoelace.

"Because the boy's **aglets** had come off his shoelaces, he had trouble lacing his shoes."

AIGUILLETTE (ay-GWUH-LET): *n.* from Fremch *aguillette* (little needle): an ornamental cord worn on the shoulder of a military uniform, as on the military aides to U.S. presidents.

"The military aide with President Obama wore an **aiguillette** over his shoulder."

AIRPLANE-BACK: *n.* the part of a cuff link that is poked through the cuff holes and then folded like the wings of an airplane.

"The **airplane-back** could barely fit through the cuff holes, making the cuff links difficult to put on properly."

BALDRIC: *n.* belt worn over the shoulder and across the chest originally to hold usually a sword, though sometimes a bugle or a drum.

"Although **baldrics** were originally designed to offer support for carrying things (especially swords), they are nowadays more likely to be part of ceremonial uniforms, like those of the University of Illinois marching band (the Marching Illini), each of whose members wears two **baldrics**, one on each shoulder."

BEAVER: *n.* the movable portion of a suit of armor that protects the mouth and chin.

"At the costume party, I went as a knight, requiring me to lift up the **beaver** to be heard."

BIRETTA: *n.* from Latin *birrus* (hooded cape): square cap with a projection on top worn by Catholic ecclesiastics.

"The **birettas** of Roman Catholic bishops are amaranth (reddish rose color), while those of priests, deacons, and seminarians are black."

CLOCK: *n.* the decoration on the side or ankles of stockings or socks.

"The **clock** on Dilbert's socks was a bit too ornate and colorful for his job interview."

COCKADE (kah-KAYD): *n.* a knot of ribbons or a rosette usually worn on the hat as a badge, as for showing allegiance to a group or cause.

"In the eighteenth century, a **cockade** was pinned on the side of a man's tricorne or COCKED HAT (*see*) or on his lapel."

COCKED HAT: *n.* a hat with a brim turned up at three places to give a three-cornered appearance; it is also known as a *tricorne*.

"On Paul Revere's head people would often see a **cocked hat**."

FOURCHETTE (FOR-shet): *n.* from French *fourchette* (fork): a strip running along the sides of glove fingers connecting the front and back of the glove.

"Because a **fourchette** was coming undone, one of my fingers was exposed to the cold."

GIBUS (JY-buhs, JAH-buhs): *n.* from *Gibus*, a nineteenth-century Parisian hatter who designed it: a collapsible opera hat that can be flattened when not in use.

"His **gibus** was held open by springs and was covered with a black, silky fabric."

GOAT'S BEARD: *n.* the small protective flap hanging down from the chin of a catcher's or umpire's mask.

"A **goat's beard** is designed to protect the throat of a catcher or an umpire."

GOOSE: *n.* in tailoring, a long-handled pressing iron weighing from eight to twelve pounds.

"The tailor insisted that a flatiron isn't heavy enough to press tailor-made garments and that a **goose** is more suitable."

HAVELOCK: *n.* from Sir Henry *Havelock*, English general in India: a light cloth covering for a military cap falling over the back of the neck.

"The British soldiers would wear **havelocks** in India to protect the backs of their necks from the sun."

JABOT (zha-BOH, JAB-oh): *n.* from French *jabot* (crop): a ruffle down the front of a shirt, blouse, or dress.

"Barbara's blouse had a **jabot** that made her look more refined than her boyfriend, who was wearing a dirty, torn T-shirt."

KAFFIYEH (kuh-FEE-yuh): *n.* an Arab headdress consisting of a square of cloth folded to form a triangle and bound on the head.

"The headdress worn by Yasir Arafat was a **kaffiyeh**."

KEEPER: *n.* the loop on a belt that keeps the end in place after it has passed through the buckle.

"David's belt began to flap because the **keeper** was torn."

KILTIE: *n.* a shoe with a long slashed tongue folding over the instep to cover the lacing.

"The woman who had just left the golf course was still wearing her **kilties**."

KLOMPEN: *n. pl.* from Dutch *klomp* (lump, wooden shoe): Dutch wooden shoes or clogs.

"Although **klompen** offer excellent protection against

falling or sharp objects, they are bad for running to a bus or anywhere else."

LAPPET: *n.* (i) a fold or flap on headgear; (ii) one of a pair of streamers of a woman's headdress usually hanging down on each side of the face; (iii) one of two flaps attached to a miter worn by a Catholic or an Anglican bishop.

"The woman had a white cap whose **lappets** she would sometimes pin on top and at other times tie under her chin."

LIFELINE: *n.* in a necktie, the thread that holds the lining in place and runs from one end to the other.

"We could tell that the **lifeline** in the tie was a good one because it had a tied loop of extra thread at each end to permit extra give."

MERKIN: *n.* a pubic wig for women, first used in the seventeenth century by prostitutes after shaving their genitalia.

"Because Kate Winslet had less pubic hair than was required for her role in the film *The Reader* (set in the 1950s), she wore a **merkin**."

MONOKINI: *n.* a topless bikini.

"The drunken customer at the Hooters restaurant asked his server to wear a **monokini** to accentuate her assets."

MOTLEY: *n.* the characteristic costume of a professional fool or jester or harlequin.

"The harlequin wore a **motley**, which included a red and black mask."

NERD PACK: *n.* plastic pouches for holding pens and pencils.

"Although doubtless many nerds wear **nerd packs**, most of them carry pencils and pens elsewhere."

PETASUS: *n.* (i) a broad-brimmed low-crown hat worn by ancient Greeks and Romans; (ii) the winged hat of the god Hermes/Mercury.

"The **petasus** on Mercury's head suggests swiftness, an appropriate attribute for a god known as a messenger."

PICKELHAUBE (**PIK**-uhl-**HOW**-buh): *n.* from German *Pickel* (pickax) and *Haube* (bonnet, cap): a spiked German helmet worn in the nineteenth and twentieth centuries by German soldiers, firefighters, and police and popularized by Otto von Bismarck.

"It is difficult to picture Otto von Bismarck without wearing a **pickelhaube**."

PLACKET: *n.* (i) a slit in a dress, blouse, or skirt, especially where the garment fastens; (ii) a pocket, especially in a woman's skirt.

"Emily put the twenty-dollar bill into the **placket** of her skirt because she didn't have her purse."

ROWEL: *n.* the revolving disk at the end of a spur with sharp points for goading horses.

"When Melissa, an advocate for animals, saw the **rowel** and its sharp points, she chided the equestrian."

SAM BROWNE BELT: *n.* from Sir *Samuel* James *Browne*, British army officer: a leather belt for a dress uniform supported by a light strap passing over the right shoulder.

"The **Sam Browne belt**, named after a British army officer serving in India, is most often seen as part of a military or police uniform."

SPORRAN: *n.* a leather pouch covered with fur and hanging in front of a Scottish kilt.

"We were told that a **sporran** was originally intended to serve as a pocket for some Scot's daily ration."

TOORIE: *n.* the little bobble atop the round, brimless Scottish cap known as the *balmoral*; the bobble is also on the wedge-shaped Glengarry headgear on the tam-o'-shanter.

"Angus's balmoral bonnet had a red **toorie** on top."

TUQUE (TUUK): *n.* from Middle French *toque* (soft hat with a narrow brim worn especially in the sixteenth century), from Old Spanish *toca* (headdress): a knitted cap, originally of wool, though now often of synthetic fibers, designed for warmth in the winter, usually tapered and sometimes having earflaps and/or a pompom.

"The Canadian wore a **tuque**, which helped keep his head warm during the winter."

TURNBACK: *n.* the part (as of a clothes hanger hook or a garment) that is turned back.

"The wooden clothes hanger had a flat body but snaky shape, with a **turnback** on the hook."

WAMUS (WAW-muhs, WAHM-uhs): *n.* a frontiersman's fringed hunting shirt, usually made of buckskin.

"When people think of Daniel Boone, they often picture him as wearing a **wamus**."

WASE (WAYZ): *n.* the circular head covering or pad used by porters when carrying loads on their heads.

"The porter put the heavy box on the **wase** he was wearing and carried it about a block."

WIMPLE: *n.* a cloth covering for the neck and sides of the face that is pinned to the hair, a band, or a hat and worn especially by nuns.

"Because the nun wasn't wearing her **wimple**, we saw her luxuriant hair."

YASHMAK (YASH-mak): *n.* a veil worn by Muslim women that is wrapped around the upper and lower parts of the face, exposing only the eyes.

"Many Westerners and others oppose the **yashmak** as excessively limiting female freedom."

~~~~~~

COLORS

~~~~~~

CANESCENT (kuh-NES-uhnt): *adj.* from Latin *canescere*, from *canēre* (to be gray, to be white), from *canus* (white, hoary): growing white, whitish, or hoary.

"Some men, including many Italians, can reach advanced years without having their hair turn gray or **canescent**."

CANITIES (kuh-**NISH**-shee-EEZ, kuh-**NISH**-eez): *n.* from Latin *canus* (white, hoary): grayness or whiteness of hair.

"Gray or white hair in women is considered a sign of age, but **canities** in men is considered a sign of distinction."

CHAMPAGNE: *n., adj.* in the world of cat fanciers, a warm honey beige shading to pale gold tan on a cat's underside.

"A **champagne** color is associated with certain cats, such as the Burmese and Tonkinese."

CHROMA (KROH-muh): *n.* the intensity, saturation, or brilliance of a color—that is, the extent to which the color is free from white or gray.

"Primary colors such as blue and red have higher **chroma** than grayish colors, such as terra-cotta or olive."

MURREY (MUHR-ee): *adj.* from Latin *morum* (mulberry, blackberry): a purplish black.

"When the apple-shaped man wore his **murrey** gym clothes, he looked like a giant mulberry."

Cooking

BARD: *v.* from French *barde* (armor for the breast of a warhorse): to cover meat or game with slices of bacon for cooking.

"The cook **barded** the lean meat to prevent it from drying out while roasting."

BROCHETTE (broh-SHET): *n.* from French, from Old French *brochete*, diminutive of *broche* (skewer, spit): a small skewer or spit used to broil or roast meat, fish, or vegetables.

"When Deena saw Tom put lamb on a **brochette**, she pointed out that she was a vegetarian."

FRANCONIA: *adj.* in cooking, a way of prepared browned potatoes, as when potatoes are placed in a pan in which meat is roasting and cooked until tender, basting frequently with the fat in the pan.

"We thought that the **franconia** potatoes nicely complemented the roast."

FRILL: *n.* a strip of paper curled out one end and rolled to be slipped over the bone of a chop in serving (*see* PAPILLOTE).

"We noticed the chef added a **frill** to the pork chop before serving it."

FRIZZLE: *v.* to fry something until it curls at the edges and becomes crisp.

"Before one **frizzles** food, it is wise to have a sharp knife or a mandolin (which has sharp blades) to produce a julienne cut."

KITCHEN STUFF: *n.* fat and grease drippings saved for later use.

"The family liked bacon grease and other **kitchen stuff** for flavoring."

O'BRIEN: *adj.* in cooking, a style of preparing sautéed vegetables (especially potatoes) with sweet peppers or pimentos.

"The **O'Brien** potatoes were diced, sautéed in butter, and dressed with chopped sweet peppers, though some recipes call for pimentos."

PAPILLOTE (PAP-uh**-LOHT):** *n.* from French *papillon* (butterfly): (i) a frilled paper cover used to decorate the bone end of a cooked chop or cutlet; (ii) a greased paper or foil wrapper in which foods (especially fish and poultry) are cooked.

"The moist fish we ate had been baked in a **papillote**."

PIPKIN: *n.* a small earthenware pot used for cooking over direct heat from coals or a wood fire.

"The **pipkin**, which was placed on a wood fire, had a horizontal handle and three feet."

RIMMER: *n.* an implement for decorating the edge of a piecrust.

"We used a **rimmer** to impress ornamental figures on the piecrust."

SCOTCH HANDS: *n.* two spatulas used for shaping butter when making it.

"The cook insisted that **Scotch hands**, which contain a ribbed or fluted side, are best when they are made from sycamore wood rather than from metal."

ZESTER: *n.* a specialized tool that removes the outer colored skin of citrus fruit (the zest).

"Because the dessert required fine shreds of lemon peel, Selma used her **zester**."

~~~~~~

CRIME

~~~~~~

RECIDIVATE (ri-SID-uh-VAYT): *v.* from Latin *recidivare* (to fall back, relapse): (i) to relapse; (ii) to fall back into criminality.

"A question criminologists study and debate is whether solitary confinement in supermax prisons makes criminals more or less likely to **recidivate** when they are released from the facility."

DATES

CYBER MONDAY: *n.* in the United States, the Monday after Thanksgiving, when online retailers supposedly have a surge in business.

"The online retailer was hoping that **Cyber Monday** would make up for a year of recession."

DEATH

CATAFALQUE (**KAT**-uh-FAWK): *n.* from Italian *cata-falco* (scaffolding): a raised platform on which a coffin lies in state during a funeral or memorial service.

"In the United States, the Lincoln **catafalque**, made of rough pine boards, has been used for all those who have lain in state in the Capitol rotunda, including not only Lincoln and several other presidents but also numerous dignitaries."

CENOTAPH (**SEN**-uh-TAF): *n.* from Greek *kenos* (empty) and *taphos* (tomb): a tomb or a monument erected in honor of a person whose body is elsewhere.

"After removing the famous man's remains, the workers erected a **cenotaph** at the original grave."

UXORICIDE (uks-OR-i-syd): *n.* from Latin *uxor* (wife) and *-cida*, from *caedere* (to kill): the murder of a wife by her husband.

"Strange as it may seem, men who now have been convicted of **uxoricide** sometimes get letters on death row from women who want to marry them."

VATICIDE (VAT-uh-**SYD**): *n.* from Latin *vates* (prophet) and *-cida*, from *caedere* (to kill): the murder, or the murderer, of a prophet.

"Because prophets can disturb people, they risk **vaticide**."

VIVISEPULTURE (VIV-uh-se-PUL-chur): *n.* from Latin *vivus* (alive) and *sepulcrum* (grave, tomb): the act or practice of burying someone alive.

"So common was the fear of accidental **vivisepulture** (*see* TAPHEPHOBIA under "Fear") in the nineteenth century that some Victorians formed an organization called the Society for the Prevention of People Being Buried Alive."

Dishware

HOLLOWARE: *n.* vessels such as bowls, cups, or vases, usually of pottery, glass, or metal with a good deal of depth and volume.

"Whereas knives and forks are flatware, bowls and cups are **hollowware**."

MONTEITH (mahn-TEETH): *n.* from *Monteith*, a seventeenth-century Scottish eccentric who wore a cloak with a scalloped hem: a large silver punch bowl with a scalloped rim.

"After the Pekingese urinated in Millie's **monteith**, the bridge players were no longer thirsty."

Doors / Windows

CRASH BAR: *n.* a mechanism for unlatching a door, consisting of a spring-loaded horizontal metal bar attached to the front of a door that opens outward; also known as a *panic bar* or a *push bar*.

"As a child, Raymond would enter the movie theater without paying because his friends would let him in by opening an exit door on which there was a **crash bar**."

DEADLIGHT: *n.* a skylight that doesn't open.

"We enjoyed the **deadlight** but were unhappy that we couldn't open it for fresh air."

DEFENESTRATE (dee-FEN-i-STRAYT): *v.* from prefix *de-* (from, down, away) and Latin *fenestra* (window): to throw out a window.

"The teacher was relieved that the window from which the students **defenestrated** him was on the first floor."

ELEPHANT DOORS: *n.* the large doors entering a TV studio.

"The **elephant doors**, when opened, were large enough to accommodate a big crowd."

FENESTELLA (FEN-uh-STEL-uh): *n.* from Latin *fenestella* (small opening or window): a small window.

"In a Roman Catholic church it is common for a **fenestella** to be in the south wall of the sanctuary near the altar."

FENESTRATED (fen-uh-STRAYD-id): *adj.* from Latin *fenestrare* (to provide with openings or windows), from *fenestra* (opening, window): provided with or characterized by windows.

"A bathroom is the one room in an apartment least likely to be **fenestrated**."

FILLISTER: *n.* the groove on the outer edge of a window frame into which glass is fitted.

"The worker who was installing the new window applied putty to the **fillister**."

INTERFENESTRAL: *adj.* situated between windows.

"We noticed the **interfenestral** painting."

JAMB: *n.* an upright that is a vertical side member of a door or window frame.

"Because the carpenter didn't correctly measure the wood for the right **jamb**, it was too short for the door."

MUNTIN: *n.* a strip of wood or metal separating and holding window panes.

"Using **muntins** and glass, builders can create a grid system dividing a single casement into small panes."

NAB: *n.* the projecting box into which a door bolt goes to hold the door.

"As soon as Dorota entered her apartment, she pushed the door bolt through the **nab**."

OCULUS: *n.* from Latin *oculus* (eye): a circular or oval window, as of a church.

"We looked through the **oculus** at the west end of the church."

PINTLE: *n.* the vertical post that runs through a door hinge.

"A drive **pintle**, often used in eighteenth-century framing when a post was used in constructing door openings, is among the strongest."

PORTCULLIS (port-KUH-luhs): *n.* from Old French *porte coleice* (sliding door): a latticed grille or gate made of wood, metal, or a combination of the two mounted in vertical grooves in castle walls and lowered by chains or ropes, acting as a last line of defense during an attack.

"Dorothy and her friends were terrified when they were inside the castle with the Wicked Witch of the West during the lowering of the **portcullis**, but in the Middle Ages residents of a castle would have felt relieved when the **portcullis** was lowered."

POSTERN: *n.* a back door or gate, allowing occupants to come and go inconspicuously, particularly in a fortification such as a city wall or castle curtain wall.

"The occupants would enter the castle through the **postern** to minimize the risk of being seen by enemies."

QUARREL: *n.* (i) a small diamond-shaped or square pane of glass in a latticed window; (ii) an arrow or a bolt shot from a crossbow.

"The young man was embarrassed when he drove a golf ball through a **quarrel** of a window."

DRINKING

BARM (bahrm): *n.* from Old English *beorma* (yeast): beer foam.

"When Buford licked the **barm** of his beer, his behavior disappointed his date."

BEER COMB: *n.* a special spatula for scooping excess foam from the tops (heads) of beer.

"Many **beer combs** resemble the familiar medical tongue depressor."

BIBULOUS (BIB-yuh-lus): *adj.* from Latin *bibulus*, from *bibere* (to drink): fond of drinking, especially excessively.

"Even though H. L. Mencken described himself as **bibulous**, he said that he would not drink until after sunset."

BILLET (BIL-uht): *n.* the thumbpiece over the hinge on the lid of a stein or a tankard.

"Because my right thumb was sore, I had trouble depressing the **billet** to open the lid of the tankard."

COMPOTATION (KAHM-poh-**TAY**-shun): *n.* a drinking or tippling together.

"The drunkard said that he never drinks before sunset and never drinks alone but does find a convivial **compotation** irresistible."

CRAPULOUS: *adj.* from Latin *crapula* (drunkenness): (i) relating to regularly overindulging in the drinking of alcohol; (ii) suffering from or due to excessive drinking or eating.

"The drunkard's ill health was due to his **crapulous** lifestyle."

GYLE: *n.* the beer produced at one brewing.

"We noticed that the beer keg carried a stenciled number representing its **gyle** to indicate its period of brewing."

JIRBLE: *v.* to pour (a liquid) unsteadily.

"The drunken party host **jirbled** out some vodka in Liz's glass."

LEGS: *n. pl.* streaks that run down the side of a glass after wine has been swirled in it.

"As the sommelier saw the pronounced streaks in my wineglass, he exclaimed, 'Good **legs**!'"

MUDDLER: *n.* a technical name for a swizzle stick, which is sometimes also called *mosser*.

"The rum drink came with a **muddler**, which we used to further mix its contents."

NEBUCHADNEZZAR (NEB-yuh-kuhd-**NEZ**-uhr, NEB-uh-kuhd-**NEZ**-uhr): *n.* the largest champagne bottle, holding about twenty times more than a standard wine bottle.

"The **Nebuchadnezzar** was more than enough champagne for our small dinner party."

NEPHALISM (NEF-uh-liz-uhm): *n.* from Greek *nēphein* (to be sober, to drink no wine): total abstinence from alcoholic beverages.

"Many people recommend that alcoholics aim for **nephalism** and not for moderate drinking."

POT-VALIANT: *adj.* valiant and bold from drunkenness.

"The **pot-valiant** man would rarely assert himself without being fortified with alcohol."

PUNT: *n.* the indentation at the bottom of a wine bottle to strengthen the bottle.

"We explained to the wine customer that the **punt** wasn't designed to reduce the amount of wine in the bottle but to protect the bottle from damage."

SCHOONER: *n.* (i) in North America, Australia, and New Zealand, a large beer glass, usually holding more than a pint; (ii) in Britain, a large glass for sherry.

"When in Boston, John had a **schooner** of his favorite beer."

TASTEVIN (TASS-tuh-van): *n.* from French *tastevin* (wine taster): a small, shallow silver cup or saucer carried by a sommelier to enable people to judge the taste of wine.

"The sommelier poured a little wine into the **tastevin** so that we could taste it."

TIPPLER: *n.* someone who often drinks alcohol, especially at regular intervals but in small amounts.

"Charlie was a **tippler** who often had a drink in his hand that he would sip throughout the day."

VERJUICE (VUR-joos): *n.* from Middle English *verjuis*, *verjus*, from Middle French *verjus*, *vert jus* (green juice): the acidic juice of crab apples or other sour fruit, such as unripe grapes.

"Melissa's lips puckered as she sipped the **verjuice**."

WORM: *n.* the business end of a corkscrew.

"Because Beth had arthritis and was weak in her hands, she had trouble manipulating the **worm** in the wine cork."

ZARF: *n.* (i) the holder for a paper cone coffee cup; (ii) an elaborate chalice-like coffee cup holder, often of silver, gold, copper, or brass.

"In Turkey, **zarfs** were developed to protect coffee cups and also people's fingers."

EDUCATION / KNOWLEDGE

CONDISCIPLE: *n.* a fellow student.

"Both Vice President Al Gore and actor Tommy Lee Jones were once not only **condisciples** but also roommates at Harvard."

EXOTERIC: *adj.* from Greek *exōterikos* (external): (i) suitable to be imparted to the public; (ii) readily comprehensible; (iii) widely known.

"The religious doctrines held by the group were for those in the inner circle and were not intended for **exoteric** consumption."

FESCUE (FES-kyoo): *n.* from Latin *festuca* (stalk, straw, rod for touching slaves in manumission): a small pointer used to point out letters or words to children or students.

"The old-fashioned teacher preferred pointing with a **fescue** instead of a laser."

INVIGILATE (in-VIJ-uh-LAYT): *v.* from Latin *inviglatus*, past participle of *invigilare*, from *in-* (in, within) and *vigilare* (to watch): to proctor an exam (especially in Britain).

"The grad student was paid to **invigilate** the undergraduate exams."

ISAGOGE (EXE-suh-GOH-jee): *n.* from Greek *eisagōgē*, from *eisagein* (to introduce): a scholarly introduction to a branch of study or research.

"The book was an excellent **isagoge** for students new to the subject but was unsuitable for grad students."

MAIEUTIC (may-YOOD-ik): *adj.* from Greek *maieutikos* (of midwifery): characterized by using the Socratic method, by which a teacher asks a series of questions to draw out from students ideas latent in their minds.

"In the **maieutic** method, the teacher is like a midwife, helping deliver not babies but ideas and knowledge inside others."

OMNILEGENT (ahm-NIL-uh-juhnt): *adj.* from Latin *omnis* (all) and *legens*, present participle of *legere* (to read): (i) reading or having read everything; (ii) characterized by encyclopedic reading.

"The poet John Milton and the historian Thomas Mac-Caulay were so learned that they appeared to be nearly **omnilegent**."

OPSIMATH (AHP-si-math): *n.* from Greek *opsimathēs* (late in learning), from *opse*, *opsi* (late) and *mathēs*, from *manthanein* (to learn): a late learner.

"Jed, who graduated from college at sixty, described himself as an **opsimath**."

PANCRATIC (pan-KRAD-ik, pan-KRAT-ik): *adj.* from Greek *pan-*, from *pas*, *pantos* (all, the whole) and *kratos* (strength, might): marked by mastery of all subjects or matters.

"Aristotle and Da Vinci revealed their **pancratic** minds in their varied accomplishments."

SCIOLIST (SY-uh-list): *n.* (i) a pretender to scholarship; (ii) one with only superficial knowledge, pretending to have a deep understanding.

"**Sciolists** can be embarrassed if they are drawn into conversation with real authorities."

SOCKDOLAGER (sahk-DAHL-uh-juhr): *n.* a decisive blow or answer.

"After looking up the answer in the *Guinness Book of World Records*, he delivered the **sockdolager**."

Energy

KUNDALINI (KOON-duh-LEE-nee): *n.* from Sanskrit *kundalinī* (snake): the yogic life force held to lie coiled like a snake at the base of the spine until aroused and sent to the head to trigger enlightenment.

"Nellie told her chiropractor, who was a student of New Age thinking, that she wasn't interested in arousing her **Kundalini;** she just wanted to relieve her back pain."

Evil

AGATHOKAKOLOGICAL (AG-uh-thoh-KAK-uh-LAH-jik-uhl): *adj.* from Greek *agathos* (good) and *kakos* (bad, harmful) and English -*logical*: composed of good and evil.

"The golfer Tiger Woods, like people generally, is neither completely good nor completely evil but **agathokakological.**"

APOTROPAIC (AP-oh-troh-**PAY**-ik): *adj.* from Greek *apotrepein* (to turn away): designed to avert or turn aside evil.

"Some people wear lucky charms to avert evil, and other people, such as the Aztecs, have committed human sacrifice for **apotropaic** reasons."

Eyewear

LORGNETTE (lorn-YET): *n.* from French *lorgner* (to take a sidelong look at): a pair of eyeglasses or opera glasses mounted on a short handle.

"Used more often as jewelry than as corrective lenses, **lorgnettes** were popular at masquerade parties and operas."

LOUPE (LOOP): *n.* a small magnifying glass used by jewelers and watchmakers.

"When the jeweler changed the band on my watch, he was looking through a **loupe**."

Fabrics

BAIZE: *n.* from French *baies*, plural of *bai* (bay-colored), probably because of its original color: a coarsely woven woolen or cotton fabric napped to imitate felt and dyed in solid colors, as in draperies, linings for furniture, and pool tables.

"Pool tables normally are covered with green **baize**."

LOFT: *n.* the resilience of springiness of wool as it comes back to shape.

"Because the wool sprung back to shape quickly, we knew that it had good **loft**."

Facial Hair

BALBO: *n.* a variation of a goatee, except that the mustache and goatee aren't connected.

"The young man, while shaving, disconnected his mustache from his goatee, creating a **balbo**."

CHINSTRAP: *n.* a beard that wraps around the chin but doesn't feature a mustache.

"Denny, who had no mustache, decided to grow a **chinstrap**."

PATRICIAN: *adj.* a beard that is almost rectangular, like the beards depicted on the Smith Brothers on the cough drop box.

"When Munson walked into the room with a long, gray **patrician** beard, we thought he was coming from a movie set depicting the Old West."

PENCIL LINE: *n.* a very narrow mustache, sometimes divided in two at the center lip.

"Jeremy's **pencil line** was so thin that it looked as if he had put it on with a pen."

TOOTHBRUSH: *n.* a thick mustache, shaved to be about an inch wide in the center, and resembling the mustaches of Adolf Hitler and Charlie Chaplin.

"Because of the notoriety of Hitler, few men nowadays sport **toothbrushes**."

WALRUS MUSTACHE: *n.* a thick, bushy mustache allowed to grow and droop over the upper and some-times even the lower lip; sometimes known as a "soup-strainer."

"If you want to know what a **walrus mustache** looks like, just look at pictures of Archduke Franz Ferdinand of Austria, President Chester A. Arthur, Mark Twain, phi-losopher Friedrich Nietzsche, George Armstrong Custer, actor Sam Elliot, Bob Keeshan (Captain Kangaroo), or musician and singer David Crosby."

Fear

AILUROPHOBIA: *n.* from Greek *ailouros* (cat) and *phobos* (fear): a morbid fear of cats.

"People who suffer from **ailurophobia** would scare cats away if they would move around and flail their arms; instead, such people usually freeze in place."

AMATHOPHOBIA (AM-uh-thuh-FOH-bee-uh): *n.* from Greek *amathos* (sand, dust): a morbid fear of dust.

"When the man suffering from **amathophobia** entered the dusty attic, he broke out in a cold sweat and ran down the stairs."

BALLISTOPHOBIA: *n.* a morbid fear of bullets, ammunition, and guns.

"A U.S. marine is less likely to suffer from **ballistophobia** than a soldier conscripted into the army."

COULROPHOBIA: *n.* from Greek *koulon* (limb), suggestive of stilts and stilt walking: a morbid fear of clowns.

"If people don't understand how the exaggerated features of clowns can inspire **coulrophobia**, they would do well to read Stephen King's novel *It* or watch the movie."

ERGOPHOBIA: *n.* from Greek *ergon* (work) and *phobos* (fear): a morbid fear of or aversion to work.

"Because Stephanie did everything she could to avoid getting a job, she was thought by some to suffer from **ergophobia**."

HYPENGYOPHOBIA (hy-PEN-jee-uh-**FOH**-bee-uh): *n.* from Greek *hypengyos* (responsible) and *phobos* (fear): a morbid fear of responsibility.

"According to many psychologists, social critics, religious leaders, and just ordinary folk, the most serious problem in America is **hypengyophobia**, which manifests itself whenever a person expects others to take responsibility for his or her choices."

TAPHEPHOBIA (**TAF**-uh-**FOH**-bee-uh): *n.* from Greek *taphē* (burial, grave) and *phobos* (fear): a morbid fear of being buried alive.

"In Poe's short story 'The Premature Burial,' the first-person anonymous narrative has **taphephobia** (*see* VIVISEPULTURE) because of his catalepsy, a condition unpredictably causing him to appear dead."

TRISKAIDEKAPHOBIA (TRIS-ky-DEK-uh-**FOH**-bee-uh): *n.* from Greek *triskaideka*, *treiskaideka* (thirteen) and *phobos* (fear): a morbid fear of the number thirteen.

"Because of **triskaidekaphobia**, it is not unusual for the thirteenth floor of a building to be called the fourteenth."

Film / TV

DUTCH ANGLE: *n.* also known as a *Dutch tilt*, *German angle*, *oblique angle*, or *Batman angle* (from the TV show), a cinematic technique in which the camera is tilted to the side so that the shot is composed with the horizon at an angle to the bottom of the frame.

"A **Dutch angle** is often used to depict the psychological uneasiness or tension in the subject being filmed, as in *Brazil* and *Edward Scissorhands*."

FOLEY: *n.* from Jack D. *Foley*, an American sound technician: a technique of producing sound effects to match specific action, as when there are footsteps.

"The technique called **Foley** involves recreating screen action to match the sound effect."

HAMMOCKING: *n.* in the TV business, inserting a less popular show between two popular ones.

"The TV executives thought that the new show needed **hammocking** to attract viewers."

MACGUFFIN: *n.* from a 1939 Alfred Hitchcock lecture at Columbia University: an object, event, or character in a film or story that keeps the plot in motion.

"In *Pulp Fiction* the briefcase retrieved by Vincent Vega and Jules Winfield is the **MacGuffin**, but in spy stories the papers revealing secrets usually serve that function."

Finance

BABY BOND: *n.* a bond having a face value less than $1,000.

"Her six **baby bonds** had a total face value of $550."

CHURNING: *n.* in stock trading, an unethical practice used by some brokers of excessively trading in a client's account to increase commissions.

"**Churning** is a breach of securities law in many jurisdictions and is generally actionable by the account holder for the return of the commissions paid and any losses resulting from the broker's choice of stocks."

GREENMAIL: *n.* the practice of purchasing enough shares in a company's stock to threaten a hostile takeover, forcing the target company to buy back the share at a premium to suspend the takeover.

"Companies that are large and undervalued or inefficient can be vulnerable to **greenmail** by investors who really don't want to own the companies but want money."

FOOD

BANTINGISM: *n.* from William *Banting*, nineteenth-century English undertaker and writer: a method of dieting by avoiding sweets and carbohydrates.

"Long before the Atkins diet there was **Bantingism**, which emphasized the avoidance of carbohydrates."

BARQUETTE (bahr-KET): *n.* from French *barquette* (small boat): a boat-shaped patty shell with a filling, such as fruit, vegetables, or custard.

"The host on the boat thought that it was appropriate to serve **barquettes**."

BASIN: *n.* the dimple at the bottom of an apple.

"He began cutting the apple at its **basin**."

BLETTING: *n.* from Old French *blet* (overripe): a process that certain fleshy fruits undergo when, after they have begun ripening, they decay and ferment.

"Some fruits, such as the Nashi pear, are at their best after some **bletting**, and others, such as the quince and persimmons, can be eaten raw only after **bletting**."

BLUMBA (BLUM-buh): *n.* a metal tag attached to meat certifying that it is kosher.

"The Jewish deli owner looked for the **blumba** before he accepted the meat as kosher."

BOLUS (BOH-luhs): *n.* a lump of soft, soggy food in one's mouth that has been ground down by one's molars.

"There is an unforgettable scene in the movie *Animal House* in which John Belushi's character turns his food into a **bolus** and then spits it out of his mouth."

CHANKING: *n.* food that is spit out, like pits, seeds, or rinds.

"Because the prunes weren't pitted, we had to put the **chanking** on our plates."

COCKLE: *n.* a small, crisp, heart-shaped valentine candy bearing a motto, such as "Love Ya."

"On Valentine's Day some schoolchildren exchanged cards and candy, especially **cockles**."

CONVIVE (kohn-VEEV, KAHN-vyv): *n.* French, from Latin *conviva* (one who lives with another, eats with another): an eating or drinking companion: a comrade at table.

"So witty and popular was the celebrity that he was considered an excellent **convive** whom people loved to invite to dinner."

DEACON: *v.* to pack (fruit or vegetables) with the finest specimen on top.

"Because the shipper had **deaconed** the apples, we didn't see any rotten apples near the top of the box."

DRAGÉE (DRA-zhay): *n.* an edible silver ball used to decorate cakes.

"**Dragées**, usually smaller than cultured pearls, look like ball bearings, though they taste much sweeter."

DREDGER: *n.* a shaker for sprinkling flour, sugar, or crumbs.

"The baker used a **dredger** to coat the doughnuts with sugar."

DUNDER (DUHN-der): *n.* the thick lees (dregs) from boiled sugarcane juice used in the distillation of rum.

"**Dunder** is the traditional source of yeast in Jamaican rum and is essential for achieving a genuine rum flavor."

ÉPERGNE (i-PURN, ay-PURN): a large table centerpiece, usually made of silver, consisting of a frame with extended arms or branches, which can hold food or candles, flowers, or ornaments.

"Traditionally, **épergnes** have been used to display side dishes, fruit, or sweetmeats."

FARCI (fahr-SEE): *adj.* from French past participle of *farcir* (to stuff, from Old French): stuffed, especially with finely ground meat.

"Because Sheila loved mushrooms and ground meat, she was delighted by the mushrooms **farci**."

FINES: *n. pl.* particles of breakfast cereals (especially sugar) at the bottom of cereal boxes obtained as a by-product of the processing.

"The little boy used to like to pour the **fines** of the cereal into a plate so he could lick them up."

FINGER: *n.* in the banana business, a single banana.

"When people buy bananas, few buy only one **finger**."

FLAVEDO: *n.* from Latin *flavus* (yellow): the colored outer peel layer of citrus fruits also called the *epicarp* or *zest*.

"The **flavedo** or zest of a citrus fruit contains the oil sacs and hence the aromatic oils."

FLETCHERIZE (FLECH-ur-YZ): *v.* from Horace *Fletcher*, health advocate who recommended chewing food at least thirty times before swallowing: to reduce food to tiny particles, especially by chewing at least thirty times.

"Although it is often prudent to **fletcherize** one's food, it is unnecessary to spend a great deal of time chewing oatmeal that has been soaking in milk."

GLASSINE (gla-SEEN): *n.* from English *glass* and *-ine* (like): a strong, thin, semitransparent, resilient glazed paper resistant to the passage of air and grease, often made into small bags and used for separating food (such as smoked salmon or individual chocolates) or for protecting book jackets.

"The **glassine** was used to package the ham."

NIDOR (NY-dor, NY-duhr): *n.* from Greek *knisa*, *knisē* (smell of burnt sacrifice): a strong smell, especially the smell of cooking or burning meat or fat.

"Vegetarians can become physically sick by the **nidor** at a picnic barbecue."

NUNCHEON (NUHN-shuhn): *n.* in England, a light midmorning or midafternoon snack consisting typically of bread, cheese, and beer.

"Because Leigh wasn't used to eating snacks, especially containing beer, the **nuncheon** seemed to reduce her energy."

ORT: *n.* a morsel left at a meal.

"Although the family intentionally left some **orts** on their plates for the kitchen staff, the food wasn't enough to provide much nourishment."

POSTPRANDIAL (pohst-PRAN-dee-uhl): *adj.* from Latin *post* (after) and *prandium* (late breakfast, luncheon): of, relating to, or occurring after a meal, especially dinner.

"After the meal, the men repaired to the drawing room for **postprandial** cigars."

RASHER: *n.* a slice of bacon.

"When asked how much bacon he wanted, the lumberjack said he wanted eight **rashers**."

SCOVILLE: *n.* from chemist Wilbur *Scoville*: a unit measuring the hotness of chili pepper, as defined by the amount of capsaicin it contains.

"The hottest chilies, such as habaneros, have a **scoville** rating of 200,000 or more, indicating that their extract must be diluted more than 200,000 times before the capsaicin is undetectable."

SKIRT: *n.* in the ice cream business, the little globule of ice cream appearing at the base of a scoop of ice cream on a cone.

"We bought an ice cream scooper that is supposed to avoid a wasteful **skirt**."

SPOOM: *n.* a frothy, light type of sherbet, mixed after freezing with uncooked meringue.

"Like sorbet, **spoom** is made from fruit juice, wine, sherry, or port and served in a tall glass."

TOMALLEY (tuh-MOW-ee, **TAM**-AL-ee): *n.* from Cariban origin; akin to Galibi *tumali* (sauce of lobster or crab livers): the liver of a lobster, which is the "green stuff" of cooked lobster and is to many a delicacy.

"Although Sandy likes lobster, she thinks **tomalley** looks too creepy to eat."

~~~~~~~~~~~~~~~~~~~~~~~~~~~~~

FURNITURE / FURNISHINGS

~~~~~~~~~~~~~~~~~~~~~~~~~~~~~

ANTIMACASSAR (AN-ti-muh-**KAS**-uhr): *n.* from English *anti-* and *Macassar* (a brand of hair oil): a protective covering for backs of chairs and sofas.

"We told Fonzie that because of his greasy hair, he was to sit on the chair with the **antimacassar**."

BOBÉCHE (boh-BESH): *n.* a slighted cupped collar (often crystal) placed over the socket of a candleholder to catch the drippings of a candle.

"The **bobèche** contained a good deal of melted wax because the candle had been burning for hours."

BOLSTER: *n.* a long narrow pillow or cushion filled with cotton, down, or fiber.

"Although in Western countries **bolsters** are usually placed at the heads of beds and function as head or back supports, in the Philippines, Indonesia, Malaysia, Singapore, and Thailand, **bolsters** are designed to be hugged when sleeping."

ESCUTCHEON (i-SKUHCH-uhn): *n.* from Latin *scutum* (shield): a flat plate framing a keyhole, door handle, or light switch.

"The **escutcheon** framing the keyhole looked like a cylindrical castle."

MODESTY PANEL: *n.* the name of an optional panel on the front of a woman's desk to hide her legs.

"Because of Amy's fondness for short skirts, her boss insisted that her desk should have a **modesty panel**."

PILLION (PIL-yuhn): *n.* from Latin *pellis* (skin, hide): a pad or cushion put behind a saddle chiefly for an extra rider.

"The cowboy often had his girlfriend sitting on a **pillion** behind him."

POOF POINT: *n.* the highest point (or crest) of a pillow or soft cushion when each corner (a nib) lies flat on a surface.

"We knew that the pillow had lost fluffiness because it had a lower **poof point** than it had earlier."

SPLAT: *n.* a single horizontal piece of wood, usually broad and flat, in the middle of the back of a wooden chair.

"When Jimmy rocked back in his wooden chair, it tipped over, breaking the **splat** and injuring his shoulder."

Games /
Recreations / Sports

AUNT EMMA: *n.* in croquet, a person who wastes time and talent by having a dull, conservative style of play.

"It's hard to have fun playing croquet when you're playing with **Aunt Emmas**."

BARMAID: *n.* in bowling, a pin hidden behind another pin.

"Pin 5 is a **barmaid** in 1-5."

BED: *n.* the part of a trampoline on which people jump.

"When we saw that Ralph had placed picnic benches under the trampoline **bed**, we concluded that either he wasn't using the trampoline or benches or he was mentally deranged."

BEDPOST: *n.* in bowling, a 7-10 split.

"The bowler was able to knock down the 7 pin of the **bedpost**."

BELLYWHOPPER: *n.* in baseball, a headfirst, diving slide into a base.

"The runner's **bellywhopper** was fast enough to keep him from being counted out, but it was so jarring to the runner that he threw up his lunch."

BESOM (BEE-zuhm): *n.* (i) a broom made of a bundle of twigs tied to a pole still available today as an outdoor broom but traditionally associated with witches and their flight (*see* TRANSVECTION in "Supernaturalism"); (ii) in the sport of curling, the broom used to sweep the ice from the path of a curling stone.

"Although a **besom** is the broom used to sweep ice from the path of a curling stone, many people associate the name more often with witches' brooms."

BIRLING: *n.* the sport of logrolling on water.

"It takes an agile lumberjack to participate in **birling** without quickly falling off the log."

BOOBY: *n.* the player with the lowest score (as in a card game).

"When we played gin rummy, Melvin was the **booby**."

BRACHIATION (BRAY-kee-AY-shuhn): *n.* the act of swinging from tree branch to tree branch employed by apes and monkeys or a similar movement (as when children on a playground swing from one horizontal bar to another).

"The physical education teacher told us that the quick alternating movement of the arms and hands required by **brachiation** is good for a child's body and brain."

BURLADERO (BUR-luh-**DAIR**-oh): *n.* from Spanish *burlar* (to deceive, make fun of): a wooden shield, a short distance from and parallel to the bullring wall, behind which a matador can seek shelter from a charging bull.

"Had the matador not been able to get behind the **burladero**, he would have been seriously injured by the bull."

CABER (KAY-bur): *n.* from Scottish Gaelic *cabar* (pole): a tree trunk used in a Scottish sport in which it is raised vertically and thrown for distance.

"The large Scottish man had huge arms from lifting weights and tossing **cabers**."

CARACOLE (KAR-uh-KOHL): *n.* from Spanish *caracol* (snail, spiral stair): a half turn to the right or the left performed by a horse and rider.

"The military **caracole** is thought to have been developed in the mid-sixteenth century when cavalrymen would discharge pistols after turning their mounts slightly to one side."

CAT: *n.* a draw in tic-tac-toe.

"When two persons play tic-tac-toe impeccably, the game will always end in a **cat**."

CESTA (SES-tuh): *n.* from Spanish *cesta* (basket), from Latin *cista* (box, chest): in jai alai, the narrow curved wicker basket glove used to catch and propel the ball.

"Because Dennis was angry with Nathan, Dennis cut several strands from Nathan's **cesta**."

CHEESY CAKES: *n.* bowling lanes in which strikes come easily.

"We were told that not all lanes are equally kind to bowlers and that some are hard to bowl strikes on and others are **cheesy cakes**."

CINCINNATI: *n.* in bowling, an 8-10 split.

"The bowler knocked down only the 8 pin of the **Cincinnati**."

CLEEK: *n.* the number one iron in golf; also known as a *driving iron*.

"The **cleek** has a long shape and an iron head with almost no slope, for hitting long, low drives."

CRANKER: *n.* a bowling style in which the bowler applies a great deal of spin to the arm swing.

"In throwing a **cranker**, one needs enough strength to take a big backswing."

CROSSE (KROSS): *n.* from French *crosier* (pastoral staff): the long-handled stick with a net at one end used to catch, carry, or throw the ball in lacrosse.

"The **crosse** used by male lacrosse players is longer than that used by female lacrosse players."

CRUCIVERBALIST (**KROO**-suh-VUR-buhl-list): *n.* from Latin *cruci-*, *crux* (cross) and *verbum* (word): a person adept at creating or solving crossword puzzles.

"Some **cruciverbalists** are so skillful that they can solve the *New York Times* crossword puzzle in under fifteen minutes."

DEADWOOD: *n.* in bowling, pins that have been knocked down.

"Because the bowler threw a gutter ball, he produced no **deadwood**."

DIMPLE: *n.* the tiny indentations in the surface of a golf ball.

"Although there is supposed to be a golf ball on the market with exactly 333 **dimples**, most balls sold today have between 300 and 450 (even-numbered) **dimples**."

DISGORGER: *n.* a tool for extracting a hook from a fish.

"Because the fishhook was too deep inside the mouth of the fish to be removed by hand, we used a **disgorger**."

DOGFALL: *n.* in wrestling, a fall in which both wrestlers go down together.

"In a **dogfall**, neither wrestler is given an advantage."

DORMIE: *n.* in golf, a player who leads by as many holes as are left to play.

"She was a **dormie** because she had a three-stroke lead after the fifteenth hole."

ENDERS: *n. pl.* those who turn the rope in jump rope games.

"When we were asked to jump rope, we said that we didn't have enough energy even to be **enders**."

FIELD GOAL: *n.* in bowling, a ball passing through a split without hitting either pin.

"A **field goal** in bowling, unlike one in football, scores no points."

FIANCHETTO (FEE-uh-KE-toh, FEE-uh-CHE-toh): *v.* from Italian, diminutive of *fianco* (side, flank): to develop a bishop in a chess game to the second square on the adjacent knight's file.

"When Boris moved his pawn in front of his queen's knight forward to the next square, we knew that he was preparing to **fianchetto** his bishop."

GLISSADE (gli-SAHD, gli-SAYD): *v.* from French *glissade* (slide, slip, skid): to slide in a standing or squatting position down a snow-covered slope without skis and often with an ice ax.

"When Mary **glissaded**, she would use an ice ax."

GRANDMA'S TEETH: *n.* in bowling, a random array of pins left standing.

"After the bowler knocked over three pins, he was left with **grandma's teeth**."

HONDA/HONDO: *n.* in rodeo performances, an eye at one end of a lariat through which the other end is passed to form a loop.

"The cowboy created a **honda** so that he could form a lasso."

JAWS: *n.* in croquet, the entrance to the uprights of a hoop.

"The drunken croquet player was rarely able to hit his ball through the **jaws**."

KNOB: *n.* the bottom of a baseball bat that keeps it from slipping out of a batter's hands.

"Under the handle of a baseball bat, below where the batter holds the bat, is the **knob**."

LAZARUS: *n.* from *Lazarus* of Bethany, who, according to the Bible, was restored to life by Jesus: in pinball, a ball that drains (seems lost) but then bounces into play.

"Like Lazarus of Bethany in the Gospel of John, a pinball **Lazarus** is thought dead and gone and then is restored to life."

MARTINGALE: *n.* any betting system in which players increase their stakes usually by doubling them after each loss.

"Because many gamblers think that their luck is certain to get better eventually, they resort to a **martingale**."

MEAT HAND: *n.* in baseball, the hand without the glove.

"Because the little boy had injured the arm of his **meat hand**, he shook off his baseball glove so he could throw the ball he had just caught with that hand."

MEDITERRANEAN DRAW: *n.* in archery, pulling the drawstring with three fingertips of the string hand, when the forefinger is on the string above the arrow while the middle and ring fingers are on the string below the arrow.

"In the **Mediterranean draw**, the arrow is normally placed on the left side of the bow."

MIBSTER: *n.* one who plays marbles.

"Almost all **mibsters** are children, but few mobsters are **mibsters**."

MONGOLIAN DRAW: *n.* in archery, a method of pulling the drawstring using only the thumb while the index finger and/or middle finger reinforces the grip.

"The **Mongolian draw**, traditional across the Asian steppes, extending to Korea and China, often involves a thumb ring."

MOTHER-IN-LAW: *n.* in bowling, a pin standing behind another pin, as when the 7 pin is left behind the 4 pin.

"After Jesse knocked down the 7 pin and 4 pin, he said that he knocked down a **mother-in-law**."

MULETA (moo-LAY-tuh): from Spanish *muleta* (a young female mule): a short red cape hanging from a staff used by a matador to maneuver a bull during the final passes before a kill.

"When the matador waved the **muleta**, the spectators knew that the bull would soon be killed."

NOCK: *n.* in archery, the groove at the feather end of an arrow into which the bowstring fits.

"A good archer knows that it is important for an arrow to fit securely in a **nock** before being shot."

NURDLE: *v.* in tiddlywinks, to send an opponent's wink too close to the pot to score easily.

"The player had **nurdled** his opponent's wink so well that the wink wasn't capable of scoring without violating natural law."

OCHE (AHK-ee): *n.* the line behind which dart players stand.

"The drunken man had trouble staying behind the **oche** when he was throwing darts."

PASE (PA-say): *n.* from Spanish *pase* (pass, feint): in bull-fighting, a movement of a cape by which a matador attracts a close, passing charge of the bull.

"The matador's **pase** reflected perfect timing, showing that the matador, not the bull, was in charge."

PEEVER: *n.* a stone or other flat object used in hopscotch.

"Although the **peever** in hopscotch is most often picked up during the game, in the past, in the boys' game, it was kicked sequentially back through the course on the return trip and then kicked out of the court."

PELOTON (PEL-uh-tuhn): *n.* from French *pelote* (small ball): in competitive bicycle racing, the main group of cyclists.

"When riding in a **peloton**, one would do well to steer clear of reckless drivers and to stay toward the front of the **peloton** to minimize the risk of crashes."

PETTICOAT: *n.* in archery, the white rim of the target.

"An archer gets no points for shooting an arrow into the **petticoat** of the target."

PICKET FENCE: *n.* in bowling, leaving the 1, 2, 4, and 7 pins.

"The bowler was able to knock down only pins 1 and 2 of the **picket fence**."

PINDICATOR: *n.* in bowling, a display board showing the bowler which pins remain standing after the first ball.

"The **pindicator** revealed four pins standing after the ball was thrown."

PIP: *n.* a dot on dice and dominoes to indicate numerical value.

"Because of almost constant use, some of the **pips** on the dice were barely visible."

PITON (PEE-tuhn): *n.* from French *piton* (eye bolt): in mountain climbing, a peg or spike driven into a crack to support a climber or a rope.

"Because many alpinists want to avoid damaging rocks, they avoid using **pitons** and choose other equipment kinder to rocks."

PONE: *n.* the card player who cuts the cards for the dealer.

"The **pone** is usually to a dealer's right."

POODLE: *n.* in bowling, a gutter ball.

"The bowler was embarrassed when, instead of throwing a strike, he threw a **poodle**."

PUMPKIN: *n.* in bowling, a ball with no spin.

"Because of Ray's advanced age and general weakness, he would often throw **pumpkins** down the bowling lane."

SAVATE (suh-VAT, suh-VAHT): *n.* from Old French *savate* (old shoe): a form of martial arts in which kicking as well as punching is allowed.

"Unlike the martial art Muay Thai (in which barefooted fighters may strike not only with their feet but also with the elbow and knees), **savate** fighters habitually wear shoes and may use only their feet in kicking and not their knees or shins."

SCLAFF: *n.* in golf, a stroke in which the club hits the ground before hitting the ball.

"When just learning to golf, people can be forgiven for occasionally digging up the golf course with some **sclaffs**."

SERPENTINE (SUR-puhn-TEEN, SUR-puhn-TYN): *n.* coiled and colored strips of paper (streamers) thrown and unfurled on festive occasions, such as parties and weddings.

"We threw colorful **serpentine** to celebrate New Year's Day."

SIGHTS: *n.* in billiards, the diamonds on the table rail.

"The **sights** on a pool table are used as reference points when aiming one's shot."

SITZMARK: *n.* from German *Sitzmarke*, *Sitz* (act of sitting) and *Marke* (mark, sign): in skiing, a hollow in the snow made by a skier who has fallen over backward.

"We could tell that many skiers fell because of the many **sitzmarks**."

SIX PACK: *n.* in bowling, six consecutive strikes.

"After five consecutive strikes, Sally knew that she had a chance to throw a **six pack**."

SLING: *n.* in badminton, a foul consisting of carrying the shuttle on the face of the racket instead of hitting it clearly.

"Because Amos didn't hit the shuttle but caught and held it on the racket, he was penalized for a **sling**."

SPILLIKIN: *n.* any of the strips used in jackstraws.

"In the game of pick-up sticks, each stick is a **spillikin**."

SPLASHER: *n.* in bowling, a strike in which the pins fall quickly.

"The bowler Don Carter threw more than a few **splashers** in the fifties and sixties, making strikes as cleanly and quickly as anyone else."

SQUIDGER: *n.* in tiddlywinks, the shooter (a large disc) used to pop (smaller) winks into flight.

"In tiddlywinks, the goal is to use one's **squidger** to cause one's winks to land either atop an opponent's winks or inside a pot or cup."

SWEET SPOT: *n.* the part of the barrel (thick part) of a baseball bat that is best for hitting the ball.

"The end of a baseball bat's barrel isn't part of the **sweet spot**, which is lower."

TAW: *n.* in marbles, a marble used as a shooter.

"In marbles, a **taw** is like a cue ball in pool."

VERONICA: *n.* in bullfighting, a movement of a matador's cape in which the cape is swung slowly away from the charging bull while the matador keeps his feet in the same position.

"It takes courage and finesse to execute an effective **veronica** because the matador must skillfully move away from the bull while resisting any attempt to move his own feet."

VIGORISH: *n.* probably from Yiddish, from Russian *vyigrysh* (winnings, profit): (i) a charge taken (as by a bookie or gambling) on bets; (ii) the interest paid to a money-lender.

"The bookie was guaranteed to make money on wagers regardless of the outcome because of the **vigorish**."

WHEEL SUCKER: *n.* in bike racing, a derogatory expression for someone who rides in a pack without taking a position at the front end, minimizing effort by reducing wind resistance.

"Bike racers say that **wheel suckers** stick to your butt like snot to a fingernail."

YIPS: *n.* an apparently baseless sudden loss of ability in different sports; in golf, a movement disorder, possibly including twitches or jerks that intervenes with putting.

"Golfers who have played for more than twenty-five years appear to be most prone to **yips**, resulting possibly from biochemical changes in the brain accompanying aging."

GEOGRAPHY

AIT (AYT): *n.* from Middle English *eit*, from Old English diminutive of *īg*, *īeg* (island): a small island, especially one in a river.

"When we were boating down the river, we saw some birds on an **ait**."

ARCIFINIOUS (ar-suh-FIN-ee-uhs): *adj.* from Latin *arcifinius*, probably from *arcēre* (to hold off, enclose) and *finis* (boundary): serving both as a boundary and as a defense, as rivers, mountains, and the sea.

"Switzerland has usually been safe from invaders largely because of its **arcifinious** terrain."

CISATLANTIC: *adj.* on this, the nearer, side of the Atlantic Ocean, whichever that happens to be.

"Because the location described by the word **cisatlantic** is relative to the speaker or writer, citizens of the United Kingdom and citizens of the United States can both use the word to refer to their own locations."

IRREDENTA: from Italian *irredenta* [in *Italia irredenta* (unredeemed Italy)]: a region related historically or ethnically to one state but politically subject to another.

"Because most national borders have been moved and redrawn over time, many people live in **irredentas**, which are sometimes violently taken over by nations previously in control."

KRATOGEN (KRAT-uh-jin): *n.* a region that has remained undisturbed while an adjacent area has been affected by mountain-making movements.

"During the continuing development of the eastern Andes, the **kratogen** of western Brazil has been stable."

SITUS (SY-duhs): *n.* from Latin *situs* (place, site): the original or proper position.

"Palestine is the **situs** of their Semitic industry."

THALWEG (THAL-veg, THAL-vek): *n.* from German *Tal*, *Thal* (valley) and *Weg* (way): in geography, the deepest continuous line along a valley or watercourse (such as a river).

"According to the principle of **thalweg**, the border between two states separated by a watercourse lies along the **thalweg**."

VUG (vug, vuog): *n.* from Cornish *vooga* (cave, underground chamber): a small cavity in a rock or vein, often with a mineral lining of different composition from that of the surrounding rock.

"It is possible for a **vug** to be mistaken for a clump of precious stones, especially if it is gleaming with quartz."

GOVERNMENT

ANDROCRACY (an-DRAHK-ruh-see): *n.* from Greek *andr-*, *andros* (man, male) and *-cracy* (rule): political and social supremacy of men.

"The feminist asserted that America is still an **androcracy**, though the degree of male dominance has lessened since the 1960s."

CAMARILLA (kam-uh-RIL-uh): *n.* from Spanish *camarilla* (small room): a group of unofficial, often secret, and usually scheming advisers to powerful leaders, such as kings or premiers.

"The popular conservative talk show host described leaders of certain unions and community groups as belonging to President Obama's **camarilla**."

EUNOMY (YOO-nuh-mee): *n.* from *eunomia*, from *eunomos* (having good laws): civil order under good laws.

"The president said that civil order alone isn't sufficient; we must have civil order because of **eunomy**."

KAKISTOCRACY (KAK-i-STAHK-ruh-see): *n.* from Greek *kakistos*, superlative of *kakos* (bad) and *-cracy* (rule): government by the worst people.

"In our system, politicians who are bought usually stay bought, but in a **kakistocracy** no citizen can depend on politicians except to produce bad results."

KLEPTOCRACY (klep-TAHK-ruh-see): *n.* from Greek *kleptein* (to steal) and Greek *kratos* (strength): (i) a government conducted by those who seek chiefly status and personal gain; (ii) a government characterized by rampant greed and corruption.

"In a **kleptocracy**, politicians and bureaucrats constantly punish hard work and self-discipline to reward laziness, imprudence, and greed until the economy stagnates or the masses wake up and no longer tolerate the corruption."

Hair

ELFLOCK: *n.* hair matted as if by elves.

"Because Dennis's long hair was rarely combed or washed, it contained many **elflocks**."

HIRCI (HUR-see): *n.* armpit hair.

"In America, a sustained marketing campaign against female **hirci** began in 1915, when there was an ad in the women's magazine *Harper's Bazaar* featuring a woman with her sleeveless arms flung into the air exhibiting her hairless armpits and the assertion that summer dress and modern dancing 'combine to make necessary the removal of objectionable hair.'"

HYPERTRICHOSIS (HY-pur-tri-KOH-sis): *n.* from Greek *hyper* (over, above) and *trichōsis* (growth of hair): excessive hair growth, either over the entire body or over some specific body part, such as the face.

"The circus performer Stephan Bibrowski (better known as "Lionel the Lion-Faced Man") had **hypertrichosis**, making him appear as if he had a lion's mane."

LEIOTRICHOUS (LY-uh-TRI-kuhs): *adj.* from Greek *leios* (smooth) and *trichos* (hair): having straight, smooth hair.

"Although the police had collected some hair fibers, they hadn't performed any tests on them to determine whether the hair was from the curly-haired victim or the **leiotrichous** suspect."

~~~~~~~~~~~~

Hands

~~~~~~~~~~~~

GOWPEN (GOW-puhn): *n.* two hands together in the shape of a bowl.

"Barry formed his hands into a **gowpen** as he drank from the lake."

GUDDLE: *v.* to catch (fish) with the hands by groping (as under banks or stones).

"Because the rural children couldn't afford fishing rods, they would go to the riverbank to **guddle** for trout."

~~~~~~~~~~~~~~~~~~~~~

HATRED

~~~~~~~~~~~~~~~~~~~~~

MISANDRY (mi-SAN-dree): *n.* from Greek *misos* (hatred) and *andr-*, *anēr* (man): a hatred of males.

"Although there may be hostile forms of feminism that reflect **misandry**, most feminists simply want women to be treated with dignity."

MISOGAMY (mis-AHG-uh-mee): *n.* from Greek *misos* (hatred) and *gamos* (marriage): a hatred of or an aversion to marriage.

"The lifelong bachelor denied accepting **misogamy** but said that he enormously valued his freedom and independence."

MISOLOGY: *n.* from Greek *misos* (hatred) and *logos* (word, reason, speech): a dislike, distrust, or hatred of argument, reasoning, or enlightenment.

"St. Thomas Aquinas believed that reason and faith can coexist and that accepting faith doesn't imply accepting **misology**."

MISONEISM (MIS-uh-**NEE**-izuhm): *n.* from Greek *misos* (hatred) and *neos* (new): a hatred or intolerance of something new or changed.

"Sometimes people who absolutely reject the placing of women in positions of power are sexist, though such rejection can spring also from **misoneism**."

MISOPEDIA (MIS-uh-**PEE**-dee-uh): *n.* from Greek *misos* (hatred) and *paid-*, *pais* (child): hatred of children.

"When the conservative asserted that the federal government can't afford to increase spending on medical care for children, the progressive accused him of **misopedia**."

Hearth

ANDIRON (**AND**-EYE-uhrn): *n.* one of a pair of metal supports used for holding logs in a fireplace.

"The cat quickly learned that the **andirons** were too hot to play near."

FENDER: *n.* a screen in front of a fireplace.

"We felt safer from embers after our host placed a brass **fender** in front of the fireplace."

INTERNET

DEEPNET: *n.* also called *deep web*, the *invisible web*, *dark web*, or the *hidden web*, information on the Internet that isn't part of the surface web, which is indexed by standard search engines, such as Google.

"Although Google is excellent for searching the web, it cannot access **deepnet**, which is several orders of magnitude larger than the surface web."

EGO-SURFING: *n.* searching the Internet for references to oneself.

"When John Smith went **ego-surfing** (*see* GOOGLEGÄNGER), he soon discovered that nearly all the references containing *John Smith* were to other people who happened to share his name."

GOOGLEGÄNGER: *n.* from *Google* and *Doppelgänger*: a person with the same name who shows up virtually when one Googles oneself (*see* EGO-SURFING).

"When Ella saw her **Googlegänger** on the Internet, she felt as if she had lost her uniqueness."

INTERSTITIAL ADVERTISEMENTS: *n.* advertisements that occur for only seconds as an Internet user is moving from one web page to another.

"**Interstitial advertisements** enable companies to place full page messages between the current page and the destination page."

TURKLEBAUM: from an email hoax about a fifty-one-year-old proofreader named *Turklebaum* who allegedly died at his desk and whose death was undetected for five days: any bogus Internet content, including fake virus warnings, urban legends, stock hoaxes, and scams.

"The email notification that said I had won a million dollars was a **turklebaum**."

~~~~~~~~~~~~~~~~~~~~~~

INTERPRETATION (BIBLICAL / LITERARY)

~~~~~~~~~~~~~~~~~~~~~~

ANAGOGE (AN-uh-GOH-jee): *n.* from Greek *anagein* (to lift up): (i) a literary interpretation that tries to extract a spiritual meaning from language; (ii) an interpretation of scripture (exegesis) that holds that underlying literal meaning is a secret heavenly meaning.

"Certain medieval theologians asserted that, whereas allegory occurs when a visible fact is signified by another visible fact, **anagoge** involves a visible fact leading above to a spiritual reality."

EISEGESIS (EYE-suh-JEE-sis): *n.* from Greek *eisēgeisthai* (to bring in, introduce, propose): personal or biased interpretation of a text, especially the Bible.

"The founder of the Radio Church of God and Ambassador College (later Ambassador University), Herbert W. Armstrong, often accused those who disagreed with his biblical interpretations of **eisegesis** and held that his interpretations were unmarred by personal biases."

JIGSAW PUZZLES

LOCK: *n.* in jigsaw puzzles, the resulting connection between pieces.

"In jigsaw puzzles, the goal is to place a piece into the proper VOID (*see*) to form a **lock**."

NOB: *n.* in jigsaw puzzles, the rounded projection that is inserted into a space (*see* VOID).

"The young child thought that **nobs** that didn't fit other jigsaw pieces should be forced into place."

VOID: *n.* the female part of a jigsaw puzzle piece.

"When we got to the last two jigsaw puzzle pieces, it was obvious which pieces needed to go into the remaining **voids**."

Journalism

LINDLEY RULE: *n.* in journalism, from journalist Ernest H. *Lindley*, who followed it during the Truman administration: a rule holding that deep and possibly sensitive background information may be published, provided that reporters and journalists avoid any attribution.

"Although the **Lindley rule** allows journalists access to sensitive information, it can also lead to collusion between the media and government and encourage officials to leak information or disinformation without taking responsibility for it."

Knickknacks / Novelties

BLOWOUT: *n.* a brightly colored party favor that unfurls when one blows into it.

"The **blowouts** at the child's party contained images of cartoon characters."

BOONDOGGLE: *n.* a braided leather or plastic cord used to decorate saddles and Boy Scout uniforms.

"The Boy Scout made a **boondoggle** for his uniform and another for his key chain."

DEELEY BOBBER: *n.* a hair band with two glitter balls or furry ears perched on springy antennae or "antlers."

"**Deeley bobbers**, which are said to have originated from John Belushi's 'Killer Bees' skit on *Saturday Night Live*, gained their trademark name in 1982."

~~~~~~~~~~~~~~~~~~~~~~~~~~~~~~~~~~~~~~~

LANGUAGE

~~~~~~~~~~~~~~~~~~~~~~~~~~~~~~~~~~~~~~~

AGGLUTINATION: *n.* in linguistics, the formation of new words by combining other words or word elements, as in *dis-figure-ment*.

"The word *en-camp-ment* illustrates **agglutination**."

ALITERATE (ay-LID-uhr-it, ay-LID-uhr-uht): *adj.* capable of reading but uninterested in doing so.

"In the United States, where there seem to be many more TV viewers than readers, **aliterate** people appear to outnumber illiterate people."

AMPHIBOLOGY (AM-fuh-**BAHL**-uh-jee): *n.* from Greek *amphibolos* (ambiguous): a phrase or sentence that is subject to more than one interpretation because of an ambiguous grammatical construction.

"The sentence *You'll be lucky if you can get Dan to work for you* can illustrate **amphibology** because it can be either praising Dan's industry or condemning Dan's lack of industry."

ANTIPHRASIS (an-TI-fruh-suhs): *n.* from Greek *anti-* (against) and *phrasis* (diction, speech): the usually ironic, humorous, or sarcastic use of words in senses opposite to their generally accepted meanings.

"When the libertarian said that he thought well of congressional thrift, we immediately recognized the **antiphrasis**."

APODOSIS (uh-PAHD-uh-sis): *n.* from Greek *apodidonai* (to restore, define): the main clause of a conditional sentence.

"In the sentence *If you go, I'll go*, 'I'll go' is the **apodosis**."

APOPHASIS (uh-PAH-fuh-suhs): *n.* from Greek *apophanai* (to deny): a rhetorical device by which one asserts or emphasizes something by pointedly seeming to pass over, ignore, or deny it.

"**Apophasis** can be cynically employed, especially in politics, as when candidate Smith says, 'I'll pass over the fact that candidate Jones has been accused of smoking dope at his son's parties because we needn't allow personal matters to enter politics.'"

ARGOT (AR-goh, AR-guht): *n.* from French *argot* (slang): a specialized idiomatic vocabulary peculiar to a particular group of people, especially criminals.

"We soon realized that the suspect was familiar with the **argot** of the underworld."

ASSONANCE: *n.* from Latin *assonare* (to respond to): the repetition of similar vowels in the stressed syllables of successive words.

"The phrase *tilting at windmills* illustrates **assonance**."

ASTEISM (AS-tee-IZ-uhm): *n.* from Greek *asteismos* (wit, witticism): an ingeniously polite insult.

"So crafty was Sheldon's **asteism** that Rick had no idea that he was being criticized."

ASYNDETON (uh-SIN-di-TUHN): *n.* from Greek *asyndetos* (unconnected): omission of the conjunctions that ordinarily join coordinate words or clauses.

"One of the most famous uses of **asyndeton** was that by Julius Caesar, who said 'I came, I saw, I conquered.'"

AUTONYM: *n.* in linguistics and anthropology, a name used by a group of people to refer to themselves or their language, as distinguished from a name given to them by another group.

"*Deutschland* is the **autonym** of the nation known in English as *Germany*."

BACK-FORMATION: *n.* a word formed from what appears to be its derivative.

"The verb *edit* was derived as a **back-formation** from *editor*."

BASILECT (BAS-uh-LEKT): *n.* the least prestigious dialect of a community.

"The aristocratic-looking executive considered Cockney speech a **basilect**."

BATHOS (BAY-thahs): *n.* from Greek *bathos* (depth): an abrupt, unintended transition from the exalted to the commonplace, producing a ludicrous effect.

"The slogan *For God, country, and Millard Fillmore High* illustrates **bathos** by ending with a descent in significance."

BATTOLOGY (buh-TAHL-uh-jee): *n.* from Greek *battologia* (stammering speech), from *battos* (stammerer) and *logos* (word, reason, speech): wearisome repetition of words.

"John Calvin thought that part of the Nicene Creed ('God from God, Light from Light, true God from true God') constituted **battology**, adding neither emphasis nor expressiveness to the document."

BÊTISE (bay-TEEZ): *n.* from French *bête* (beast, fool), from Old French *beste* (beast): foolish act or remark.

"The **bêtise** about wanting to have learned Latin better to be able to talk easily with Latin Americans was never uttered by former Vice President Dan Quayle but was part of a joke told by a Republican politician and ascribed to Mr. Quayle."

BILLINGSGATE: *n.* from *Billingsgate*, a former fish market in London, England, known for abusive language: foul, abusive language.

"The **billingsgate** used to condemn a local politician was considered too coarse for the formal dinner."

CATACHRESIS (kat-uh-KREE-sis): *n.* from Greek *katachrēsthai* (to misuse): strained, paradoxical, or incorrect use of a word, either in error (as when *infer* is used to mean *imply*) or by intention (as when an author intentionally uses a mixed metaphor).

"When Barbara said that John's words 'inferred a belief' in her guilt, she noticed the **catachresis** and wished that she had said 'implied a belief.'"

CHIASMUS (ky-AZ-muhs): *n.* from Greek *chiasmos*, from *chiazein* (to mark with a chi): a rhetorical figure in which the second half of an expression is balanced against the first with the parts reversed.

"President Obama used **chiasmus** when he said, 'My job is not to represent Washington to you but to represent you to Washington.'"

COUNTERWORD: *n.* a word (such as *cool*, *great*, and *swell*) that has acquired such a broad and vague range of meaning through widespread use in many markedly different contexts that it is almost meaningless.

"The young man's language consisted almost entirely of **counterwords**, including *sweet*, *awful*, and *cool*."

CURTAIN LECTURE: *n.* a censorious lecture by a wife to her husband in privacy, often in bed.

"Doubtless many unfaithful men receive some **curtain lectures**, especially before divorces."

DEFINIENDUM (di-FIN-ee-EN-duhm): *n.* from Latin, neuter of *defiendus*, gerundive of *definire* (to define, determine, explain): whatever is being defined as an entry in a dictionary.

"When lexicographer Samuel Johnson defined *network* as 'anything reticulated or decussated, at equal distances, with interstices between the intersections,' his definition was much more obscure than the **definiendum**."

DEFINIENS (duh-FIN-ee-ENZ): *n.* from Latin, present participle of *definire* (to define, determine, explain): the word or words serving to define another word or expression, as in a dictionary.

"In producing a **definiens** of a word, one should avoid using words that are more obscure than the word that is to be defined (*see* DEFINIENDUM)."

DIACOPE (dy-**AK**-uh-PEE): *n.* a rhetorical device in which a word or phrase is repeated after an intervening word or phrase for emphasis.

"In Psalm 75:1 (New American Standard Bible translation), there appears a **diacope**: 'We give thanks to Thee, O God, we give thanks.'"

DITTOGRAPHY (di-TAHG-ruh-fee): *n.* from Greek *dittos* (double) and *-graphy* (writing): the (usually unintentional) repetition of letters, syllables, words, or phrases in writing.

"When little children write 'rememember' for *remember*, and young adults write 'philososophy' for *philosophy*, they are producing **dittography**."

DYSPHEMISM: *n.* a disagreeable, offensive, or disparaging expression for an agreeable or inoffensive one.

"The customer used the **dysphemism** 'axle grease' to refer to butter."

EMBOLOLALIA (EM-buh-loh-**LAY**-lee-uh): *n.* from Lati *embol-*, *embolismus* (intercalation) and Greek *lalia* (chatter, prattle): insertion of meaningless sounds or vacuous words into speech, especially as fillers.

"When Bobby gave his oral book report, he added *you know*, *um*, and *uh* so often that our condescending English professor shouted, 'Cut out the **embololalia**, Baa-Baa-Bobby.'"

EPENTHESIS (i-PEN-thi-sis): *n.* from Greek *epenthithenai* (to insert a letter): the insertion of one or more extra sounds into a word, especially in the interior of the word.

"When the coach said, 'My best *athalete* lives with his *hampster* on *Ellum* Drive,' we knew that he had a problem with **epenthesis**."

EPIDEICTIC (ep-uh-DYK-tik): *adj.* from Greek *epideiknynai* (to display): designed primarily for rhetorical effect, as in speech for ceremonial ovations of praise and blame.

"The awards ceremony at the Kennedy Center predictably included high-flown, **epideictic** speeches."

EPIZEUXIS (EP-i-ZOOK-sis): *n.* from Greek *epizeuxis* (act of fastening together), from *epizeugnynai* (to fasten together): a figure of speech by which a word is repeated with vehemence or emphasis.

"In *Hamlet*, Hamlet uses **epizeuxis** when he says, 'Words, words, words,' and in *King Lear*, Lear uses **epizeuxis** when he says, 'No, no, no, no!'"

EUONYM (YOO-uh-NIM): *n.* a name well suited to the person, place, or thing named.

"Chris Moneymaker has a **euonym** because he paid $39 to sit at the 2003 poker world series and won the $2,500,000 grand prize."

EXONYM (EK-soh-nim): *n.* a name by which one group or social group refers to another and by which the group so named doesn't refer to itself.

"The English name *Charles* is an **exonym** of *Karl* in German."

EXORDIUM (eks-OR-dee-uhm): *n.* from *exordiri* (to begin, begin a web, lay a warp): the introductory part of a discourse or composition.

"The author expressed the organization of his essay in the **exordium**."

EYE DIALECT: *n.* originally from George Philip Krapp, who, in *The English Language in America*, used the expression to describe spellings that violate a convention "of the eyes, not of the ear": intentional use of nonstandard spelling to draw attention to either pronunciation or the speaker's nonstandard (possibly uneducated or foreign) dialect.

"Mark Twain, Joel Chandler Harris, and William Faulkner all used **eye dialect** to highlight nonstandard dialects."

GRAMMALOGUE: *n.* a word expressed as a sign, such as *&* for *and*.

"The symbols *&*, #, and @ are all **grammalogues**."

HAPLOGRAPHY (hap-LAHG-ruh-fee): *n.* from Greek *haplo-* (single) and *-graph* (writing): the accidental omission of a letter or letter group that should have been repeated in writing.

"When people write 'mispell' for *misspell*, they're guilty of **haplography**."

HETEROLOGICAL: *adj.* of a word or phrase not possessing the property it describes.

"Because the words *German* and *monosyllabic* don't describe themselves, they are **heterological**."

HOLOPHRASIS (huh-LAHF-ruh-suhs): *n.* from Greek *holos* (whole, entire, all) and *phrasis* (expression, phrase):

a prelinguistic use of a single word to express a complex idea, memorized by rote and used without grammatical intent, as when an infant says "Up" to convey "Pick me up."

"When **holophrasis** is combined with body language, context, and tone of voice, it is usually sufficient to express a child's needs, as when a child says 'Cookie' for 'Give me a cookie.'"

HOMONYM: *n.* from Latin *homonymum*, from Greek *homōnymon*, from neuter of *homōnymos* (having the same name): a word that is the same in spelling and pronunciation as another but different in meaning.

"**Homonyms** can promote wordplay, as when conservatives defend the right to bear arms while liberals defend the right to arm each bear."

HORTATORY (**HAWR**-tuh-TAWR-ee, **HAWR**-tuh-/TOHR-ee): *adj.* from Late Latin *hortatorius*, from Latin *hortatus*, past participle of *hortari* (to extort): marked by exhortation or strong urging.

"President Obama's **hortatory** speeches of change and hope helped him win the election."

HYPERURBANISM: *n.* a form, pronunciation, or usage that overreaches correctness to avoid provincial speech.

"When the secretary said 'between you and I' and 'Whom shall I say is calling?,' she was accused of **hyperurbanism** by her verbally obsessed boss."

HYPOCORISM (hy-**PAHK**-uh-RIZ-uhm, HY-puh-KOR-IZ-uhm): *n.* from Greek *hypokorisma* (endearing name): a pet name, especially a diminutive or abbreviated form of someone's full name.

"*Billy* is a **hypocorism** for *William*."

IDIOLECT (ID-ee-uh-LEKT): *n.* from Greek *idios* (personal, peculiar) and *dialect* (language unique to a group of people): a variety of a language (as measured, for example, by vocabulary, grammar, and pronunciation) unique to an individual.

"Forensic linguists try to identify whether a particular person produced a given text by comparing the style of the text with the **idiolect** of the person."

ILLEISM (IL-ee-IZ'M): *n.* from Latin *ille* (he, that, one, that) and English -*ism*: (i) excessive use of the pronoun *he*, especially in speaking of oneself; (ii) the habit of speaking of oneself in the third person.

"When Malcolm engaged in **illeism**, he was still constantly talking about himself but was simply not saying 'I.'"

IPSE DIXIT (IP-see **DIK**-sit): *n.* from Latin *ipse dixit* (he himself said it), originally from Greek in reference to statements made by Pythagoras and accepted without question by his followers: an assertion made on authority but not proved.

"The talk show host asserted that no one should accept his **ipse dixit** but should check out his contentions."

LITOTES (**LY**-tuh-TEEZ, **LYD**-uh-TEEZ, ly-TOHD-eez): *n.* from Greek *litotēs*, from *litos* (simple, plain): a figure of speech consisting of an understatement in which an affirmative is expressed by negating its opposite.

"When people describe a great pianist as 'not a bad pianist,' they are using **litotes**."

LOGOMACHY (loh-GAH-muh-kee): from Greek *logomachia*, from *log-* (word, thought, speech) and *machesthai* (to fight): a dispute over or about words.

"A **logomachy** can lead to violence, especially when the words involve politics or religion."

LONGUEUR (lawng-GUR): *n.* from French *longueur* (length), from Old French *longour*, from *lonc, long* (long), from Latin *longus* (long): a dull and tedious section, as of a book or play.

"Our psychology text, despite its **longueurs**, taught us a good deal."

MERISM: *n.* from Greek *meros* (part): in rhetoric, a figure of speech by which a single thing is described by a conventional phrase that names several of its parts or all its parts.

"**Merisms** are common in the Bible, as when in Psalm 139:2 (King James Version), the psalmist declares that God 'knowest my downsitting and mine uprising,' implying that God knows all that the psalmist does."

MERONYM: *n.* from Greek *meros* (part) and *onoma* (name): a word naming a part of a larger whole, as when *brim* and *crown* are meronyms of *hat.*

"The word *finger* is a **meronym** of *hand.*"

METONYMY (muh-TAHN-uh-mee): *n.* a figure of speech in which one word or phrase is substituted for another with which it is closely associated, as when the phrase *Oval Office* is used to describe the positions or functions of the U.S. president.

"When servers at a restaurant say that the tuna salad sandwich left without paying, they are using **metonymy**."

MONDEGREEN: *n.* from American author Sylvia Wright in her essay "The Death of Lady Mondegreen": the mishearing or misinterpretation of a phrase, typically in a poem or a song, in a way that yields a new meaning to the phrase.

"When Joan Baez covered the Band's song 'The Night They Drove Old Dixie Down,' she produced a **mondegreen** by singing, 'Like my father before me, I'm a working man,' instead of the original line 'Like my father before me, I will work the land,' changing the narrator, Virgil Caine, from a farmer to a laborer."

MONEPIC (MAH-nep-ik, MOH-nep-ik): *adj.* from Greek *monos* (one) and *epos* (word): consisting of one word or of sentences of one word.

"No general was ever more succinct than General Anthony Clement McAuliffe, who, when besieged by Germans at the Battle of Bastogne and asked to surrender, replied with a **monepic** 'Nuts!'"

PALILOGY (puh-LIL-uh-jee): *n.* a figure of speech in which a word or phrase is repeated for emphasis.

"When the preacher talked about adultery, he used **palilogy**, calling it 'sin, sin, sin.'"

PARALIPSIS (PAR-uh-**LIP**-sis): *n.* from Greek *paraleipsis* (neglect, passing over), from *paraleipein* (to leave aside): a rhetorical trick by which the speaker or writer emphasizes something by professing to ignore it, as when people say or write "not to mention," "to say nothing of," "leaving aside," or "far be it from me to mention."

"When the senator said that he would not deign to mention his opponent's problems with honesty, we saw the **paralipsis** as a personal attack."

PARISOLOGY (PAR-ah-**SAHL**-uh-jee): *n.* from Greek *parisos* (almost equal, even balanced) and *-logy* (word, reason, speech, account): the use of equivocal or ambiguous words.

"Many politicians find safety in **parisology** rather than in straightforward, unequivocal language."

PEJORATION: *n.* from Late Latin *pejorare* (to worsen): in linguistics, a gradual worsening of meaning, as when a word becomes derogatory or increasingly disparaging.

"The word *silly* used to mean 'happy,' 'blissful,' and 'fortunate,' but underwent **pejoration**, as it came to mean, in the 1500s, first 'weak' and 'insignificant' and then gradually 'lacking good sense,' 'foolish,' and 'empty-headed.'"

PENULT (PEE-nuwt, pi-NUHLT): *n.* from Latin *paenultima*, feminine of *paenultimus* (next to last): the next-to-last member of a series, especially the next-to-last syllable of a word.

"The **penult** of *teacupful* is 'cup.'"

PERORATION: *n.* from Latin *perorare* (to argue a case to the end, bring a speech to a close): the concluding section of a speech.

"The speaker saved his best lines for the **peroration**."

PHATIC (FAT-ik): *adj.* from Greek *phatos* (spoken), from *phanai* (to speak): (i) of, relating to, or being speech used to share feelings or to establish a sociable mood rather than to communicate ideas or information; (ii) pertaining to small talk.

"Asking people how they are is usually not a request for detailed information but a social lubricant, an example of **phatic** communication."

PILCROW (PIL-kroh): *n.* from probably alteration of Middle English *pylcrafte*, modification of Late Latin *paragraphus*: a mark signifying a paragraph (¶).

"The English teacher put **pilcrows** where students should have begun new paragraphs."

PLEONASM: *n.* from Greek *pleonazein* (to be more, to be in excess, to be redundant): excessive verbiage, especially through redundant language.

"When author Raymond Chandler in *The Big Sleep* used the expression 'poodle dogs,' he was using a **pleonasm**."

POLYSEMOUS (PAHL-ee-SEE-muhs): *adj.* from Late Latin *polysemus*, from Greek *polysēmos*, from *poly-* (many) and *sēma* (sign, token, seal): having multiple meanings.

"The words that are the most **polysemous** in the *Oxford English Dictionary* are *set* and *look*, though some dispute their relative order."

PROTASIS (PRAHT-uh-sis): *n.* from Greek *proteinein* (to stretch out before, to put forward): the dependent clause of a conditional sentence.

"In the sentence *If I'm invited, I'll go,* 'If I'm invited' is the **protasis**."

PUFFERY: *n.* extravagant advertising claims.

"Some ads contain so much **puffery** that one would think that the product could make heaven unnecessary."

RHINESTONE VOCABULARY: *n.* words and phrases speechwriters or politicians use to appeal to particular groups.

"The expressions *family values*, *Wall Street fat cats*, *big oil*, *need for diversity*, and *need to give back* are all part of a **rhinestone vocabulary**, useful for appealing to political constituencies."

SCHOLASM (SKOH-laz-um): *n.* from *scholastic*: a pedantic or academic expression.

"The first-year college students found it difficult to understand the professor's **scholasms**."

SCHWA (SHWAH): *n.* an unstressed vowel represented by an inverted e- (ə), such as the sound of the first and last vowels of the English word *American* or the sound of the last vowel in the German name *Nietzsche* or *Porsche*.

"A friend related that he knew of at least one case in which a salesperson was fired for failing to pronounce the word *Porsche* with a **schwa** at the end."

SHERMAN STATEMENT: *n.* from American Civil War General William Tecumseh *Sherman*, who, when he was being considered as a possible Republican candidate for the presidential election of 1884, declined by saying, "I will not accept if nominated and will not serve if elected": a clear and direct statement by a potential candidate that he or she won't run for a particular elected position.

"Although in June 2004, Scottish National Party former leader Alex Salmond issued what appeared to be a **Sherman statement** ("If nominated I'll decline, if drafted I'll defer, and if elected I'll resign"), a month later he changed his mind and still later became the first minister of Scotland."

SYNCATEGOREMATIC (sin-KAT-i-GUR-uh-**MAT**-ik): *adj.* (i) incapable of standing alone as a term in a proposition; (ii) having significance only in connection with another expression.

"Because *right* and *down* have meaning only in relation to other words with which they are contrasted, they are **syncategorematic** expressions."

SYNECDOCHE (si-NEK-duh-kee): *n.* from Greek *synekdochē* (simultaneous understanding, interpretation): a rhetorical figure in which a part is used to represent the whole, the whole for a part, the specific for the general, the general for the specific, or the name of the material for the thing made.

"When naval officers say, 'All hands on deck,' they are using **synecdoche**."

TAPINOSIS (tap-in-OH-sis): *n.* from Greek *tapeinos* (low, humble, poor): the use of undignified language or names to depreciate or debase persons or things.

"Calling the Mississippi River 'a stream' is engaging in **tapinosis**."

TAUTONYM (TAWT-uh-nim): *n.* a taxonomic designation, such as *Gorilla gorilla* or *Mephitic mephitic* (a North American skunk), in which the genus and species names are the same.

"Although **tautonyms** are used in zoology (as in *Vulpes vulpes*, the red fox), they are no longer accepted in botany."

TITTLE: *n.* from Latin *titulus* (title): (i) a tiny amount or part of something; (ii) a point or small sign used as a diacritical mark in writing or printing; (iii) the dot in the letter *i* and *j*.

"We mustn't forget to cross every *t* and put a **tittle** on every lowercase *i* and *j*."

TOPONYM: *n.* a place name—that is, the name of a geo-graphical locality (as of a city or town).

"Because the **toponyms** *Norfolk* and *Suffolk* are related to 'north folk' and 'south folk,' it isn't surprising to find Norfolk north of Suffolk on a map, whether in England or in Virginia."

TROPE (TROHP): *n.* from Greek *tropos* (turn, way): a figurative or metaphorical use of a word or expression.

"When Jesus called Peter a rock, he was using a **trope**."

ULTIMA (UL-tuh-muh): *n.* from Latin, feminine of *ulti-mus* (last): the last syllable of a word.

"The **ultima** of *female* is 'male.'"

WEGOTISM (WEE-guht-IZ-uhm): *n.* from *we* and *ego-ism*: excessive use of *we* by a speaker or writer.

"Dennis's **wegotism** became ridiculous when he said, after someone stepped on his toes, 'We don't like people stepping on our toes.'"

WING: *n.* a Slavic mark over the letter *c* to indicate that it is to be pronounced *tch*.

"The name *Čapek*, as in the name of the author Karl Čapek, who invented the word *robot*, is spelled with a **wing**."

XENOGLOSSIA: *n.* from Greek *xenos* (stranger) and *glossa* (tongue, language): the putative paranormal ability to speak or write a language that couldn't have been ac-quired by natural means.

"Whether **xenoglossia** has ever happened in real life, it has definitely occurred in movie scripts, as when a demonically possessed child speaks flawless medieval Latin."

YINGLISH: *n.* from a blend of *Yiddish* and *English*: English marked by numerous borrowings from Yiddish.

"In the 1920s through the 1960s, the summer resorts of the Catskill Mountains included many Jewish comedians whose jokes used **Yinglish**."

~~~~~~~~~~~~~~~~~~~~~~~~~~~~~~~~~~~~~~~

LAW

~~~~~~~~~~~~~~~~~~~~~~~~~~~~~~~~~~~~~~~

ASPORTATION: *n.* from Latin *asportatus*, past participle of *asportare* (to carry off): felonious removal of goods.

"The store manager asked the workers to avoid stopping the shoplifter until she had left the store so that the store could more easily prove **asportation**."

ATTRACTIVE NUISANCE DOCTRINE: *n.* in law, the tort doctrine stating that landowners may be held liable for injuries to children trespassing on their property if the injury is caused by hazardous objects or conditions that are likely to attract children unable to appreciate the risk posed by the object or condition.

"We told our neighbor that he needed to fence in his swimming pool, or else he could be liable for injuries to trespassing children because of the **attractive nuisance doctrine**."

BARRATRY (BAR-uh-tree): *n*. from Middle French *baraterie* (deception): the practice of persistently instigating lawsuits, typically groundless.

"A fictional character named Steve Bozell, created by radio comic and voice impersonator Phil Hendrie, was guilty of **barratry**, as when he sued the Parks and Recreation Department of Riverside, California, for putting a blue dye into a public swimming pool that activated when Mr. Bozell urinated in the pool, causing him great embarrassment."

CIVIL DEATH: *n*. total deprivation of civil rights, as from a conviction for treason or any crime resulting in life imprisonment.

"Some murderers serving life sentences make all sorts of demands about how they want to be treated in prison as if they haven't suffered **civil death**."

CONTUMACY: *n*. from Latin *contumacia* (stubbornness, obstinacy): stubborn resistance to authority, especially in willful contempt of court.

"Judge Judy never has tolerated **contumacy** in her court."

EMBRACERY: *n*. the act of one who attempts to influence a juror corruptly to sway a verdict in a trial, as by promises, money, or threats.

"In the movie *The Juror* the character Mark Cordell (Alec Baldwin) commits, among other crimes, **embracery** as he threatens to kill juror Annie Laird (Demi Moore), her son, and another person."

GRAVAMEN (gruh-VAY-muhn): *n.* from Latin *gravare* (to burden): (i) the part of an accusation that weighs most heavily against the accused; (ii) the most important part of a grievance.

"We asked Zelda to forget the less important parts of her grievance and give us only the **gravamen**."

MALVERSATION (MAL-vur-**SAY**-shuhn): *n.* from Middle French, from *malverser* (to misbehave), from Old French, from Latin *male versari*, from *male* (wrongly, ill) and *versari* (to behave, conduct oneself): corruption in a position.

"Vice President Spiro Agnew, who worked for the only American president (Richard Nixon) to resign, was himself forced to resign because of **malversation:** he pleaded 'no contest' to having received bribes."

MURDRUM (MUR-drum): *n.* from Old French *murdre* (murder): (i) a murder in secret; (ii) a fine paid to Norman kings by the village where a person was killed unless the killer was produced or proof was given that the slain person was not a Franco-Norman.

"The homicide was probably a contract killing—a **murdrum** lacking both witnesses and traces of evidence."

PETTIFOGGER (PET-uh-FAW-gur): *n.* from *petty* and obsolete English *fogger* (underhand dealer), probably from *Fugger* (a German family of merchants in the fifteenth and sixteenth centuries): a lawyer whose methods are petty, underhanded, or disputable.

"The panel called for a cap of $250,000 on noneconomic damages in medical malpractice suits to reduce medical costs produced by lawyers, especially **pettifoggers**."

Marriages /
Relationships

EXOGAMY (eks-AHG-uh-mee): *n.* from Greek-derived *ex-* (out of, without) and *-gamy* (marriage, union): marriage outside a specific group, especially when contrary to custom or law.

"The Jewish man worried that his heritage may become difficult to preserve because of **exogamy**."

HYPERGAMY (hy-PUR-guh-mee): *n.* from Greek *hyper* (over, above) and *gamein* (to marry): marriage into an equal or higher caste or social group: "marrying up."

"When the peasant married the prince, she knew that her **hypergamy** would benefit her children."

MISOGAMY (*see* "Hatred").

OPSIGAMY (ahp-SIG-uh-mee): *n.* from Greek *opse, opsi* (late) and *gamos* (marriage): marriage late in life.

"Because Irwin was single until he was close to fifty, his **opsigamy** surprised some people."

MATH

ALGORISM (AL-guh-RIZ-uhm): *n.* the system of Arabic numerals.

"**Algorism** is much more useful than Roman numerals, which lack a zero."

ALIQUOT (AL-i-KWAHT): *adj.* from Latin *aliquot* (some, several): dividing into something exactly.

"The number *3* is an **aliquot** part of the number *12*."

LEMNISCATE (lem-NIS-kuht): *n.* from Latin *lemniscatus* (with hanging ribbons): the symbol for infinity, which resembles the figure 8 on its side (∞).

"In the 1993 movie *The Vanishing*, Jeff Bridges was a serial killer and math professor who wore a metallic **lemniscate** as jewelry."

MINUEND (MIN-yoo-END): *n.* from Latin *minuendum* (thing to be diminished), from *minuere* (to lessen): a number from which another number is subtracted.

"In the equation $35 - 15 = 20$, the **minuend** is *35*."

SUBTRAHEND: *n.* a quantity that is subtracted.

"In the equation $10 - 6 = 4$, 6 is the **subtrahend** (*see* MINUEND)."

VINCULUM (VIN-kyuh-luhm): *n.* from Latin *vincire* (to tie, fasten): a horizontal line above two or more members of a compound mathematical expression to show that the expression is to be treated as a single term, such as $\overline{a + b + 2}$.

"A **vinculum** has the same grouping function as parentheses, brackets, and braces (*see* BRACE under "Punctuation Marks")."

Measurements / Quantities

BARLEYCORN: *n.* one third of an inch.

"The eraser atop my pencil is about a **barleycorn** in length."

BUNDLE: *n.* a unit of measurement equal to 1,000 sheets of writing paper.

"Because each of us needed 500 sheets of paper, we bought one **bundle**."

CHAIN: *n.* a unit of measure equal to twenty-two yards or sixty-six feet.

"When you walked one statute mile, you walked eighty **chains**."

DASH: *n.* originally a small liquid measure of indefinite amount, though more recently a liquid and dry measure for which several companies have created tiny measuring spoons holding ⅛ teaspoon.

"I told Sarah that if she were going to sweeten my coffee with a **dash** spoon, she'd need to fill up the spoon sixteen times because I usually take two teaspoons of sugar."

FRAIL: *n.* (i) basket for holding dried fruit (especially raisins or figs); (ii) the weight of a frail (basket) full of raisins or figs (between fifty and seventy-five pounds).

"We gave the workers at the clinic a **frail** of raisins."

GILL: *n.* a unit of measure equal to four fluid ounces.

"A pint contains four **gills**."

GREAT GROSS: *n.* twelve gross (12 × 144) or 1,728 of some article.

"When the hot-dog-eating champion was asked how many hot dogs he had eaten in the last six months, he said, 'I don't know, but the number is at least a **great gross.**'"

HAND: *n.* (i) in the banana business, a bunch of bananas; (ii) a measure of the height of horses equivalent today to four inches.

"After Sheryl took the bananas out of the bag, she removed one from the **hand** to give to her daughter."

HOGSHEAD: *n.* in the United States, a unit of measure equal to 63 gallons of alcoholic beverage, such as wine or ale.

"The partygoers drank a **hogshead** of ale."

HOLUS-BOLUS (HOH-lus BOH-luhs): *adv.* all at once.

"If we hadn't moved the furniture **holus-bolus** into storage, it would have taken forever to complete the move."

NOGGIN: *n.* a small quantity of drink usually equivalent to a GILL (*see*), that is, four ounces.

"The bartender poured the woman a **noggin** of rum."

PINCH: *n.* originally "an amount that can be taken between the thumb and forefinger" but without any definite equivalent in other units of measure, though more recently a measure for which several companies have created spoons holding $\frac{1}{16}$ teaspoon.

"According to some current authorities, a DASH (*see*) is $\frac{1}{8}$ teaspoon, and a **pinch** is $\frac{1}{2}$ dash."

ROD: *n.* a unit of length equal to 5.5 yards or 16.5 feet or $\frac{1}{320}$ of a statute mile.

"If the offense in American football gains at least one yard less than two **rods** within a series of four plays, it gains a first down."

SMIDGEN: *n.* originally a small, indefinite amount, though more recently a measure for which several companies have created measuring spoons holding $\frac{1}{32}$ teaspoon.

"According to some authorities, a pinch is $\frac{1}{16}$ teaspoon and a **smidgen** is $\frac{1}{2}$ pinch."

TARE WEIGHT: *n.* the officially accepted weight of an empty car, vehicle, or container that, when subtracted from the gross weight, yields the net weight of the cargo or shipment upon which charges are calculated.

"Because officials knew the **tare weight** of the trailer, they were able to calculate the weight of its cargo."

TOD: *n.* a unit of weight for wool equal to about twenty-eight pounds (12.7 kilograms).

"We bought a **tod** of wool to make some sweaters."

Measuring Devices

BRANNOCK DEVICE: *n.* from Charles F. *Brannock*, inventor of the device: the metallic foot-measuring device in shoe stores that measures a foot from heel to toe, the arch of the foot, and the width of the foot.

"The **Brannock device** allows one to measure both the length and the width of a foot."

KONIMETER (koh-NIM-i-tuhr): *n.* from Greek *konia* (dust) and English *-meter*: an instrument for measuring the amount of dust in the air.

"The cleaning crew had masks when they used a **konimeter** to measure the dust in the hoarder's home."

OROMETER: *n.* from Greek *oros* (mountain) and English *-meter*: a type of barometer used for measuring the height of mountains above sea level of the place where the observation is made.

"By using an **orometer** the scientists determined the height of the local mountains."

SNELLEN CHART: *n.* from Dutch ophthalmologist Herman *Snellen*, who developed the eye chart during 1862: an eye chart, traditionally with eleven lines of block letters that grow in number and decrease in size.

"When the patient couldn't see beneath the third line of the **Snellen chart**, we knew it was time for a new prescription for his glasses."

SPHYGMOMANOMETER (SFIG-moh-muh-**NAH**-muh-tuhr): *n.* from Greek *sphygmos* (pulse), from *sphyzein* (to throb), *manos* (sparse), and English *-meter*: an instrument for measuring blood pressure in the arteries, especially one with a pressure gauge and a rubber cuff that wraps around the upper arm and inflates to constrict the arteries.

"The bodybuilder's arms were so large that the nurse couldn't fit the cuff of the **sphygmomanometer** around his arm."

WAIST: *n.* the most narrow part of an hourglass.

"The **waist** of an hourglass is clearly the smallest part."

MEDICAL CONDITIONS

ACOUSMA (uh-KOOZ-muh): *n.* from Greek *acousma* (something heard), from *akouein* (to hear): a nonverbal auditory hallucination such as a buzzing or a ringing.

"The buzzing in her ear was not caused by anything outside her but was **acousma**."

BRUXISM (BRUHKS-IZ-uhm): *n.* from Greek *brychein* (to gnash the teeth).

"The dentist told me that I was either chewing on rocks or suffering from **bruxism**."

BURGER: *n.* in skateboarding, a bad bruise or scrape.

"Although Jeff's legs are now free from bruises and scrapes, they contained several **burgers** when he was learning to skateboard."

CADUCITY: *n.* from French *caducité*, from *caduc* (falling, decrepit), from Latin *caducus* (ready to fall, falling): weakness from age.

"The physician asserted that **caducity** is much more of a threat to those who don't exercise, eat right, or have positive attitudes than it is to those who treat their bodies and minds responsibly."

CHORDEE (KOR-dee): *n.* from French *cordée*, feminine of *cordé* (corded): a downward bowing of the head of the penis, possibly congenital though often from gonorrhea.

"The physician told us that **chordee**, most noticeable during an erection, may result from an arrest of penile development during an early stage of the fetus."

DIASTEMA (DY-uh-STEE-muh): *n.* the gap between teeth in a jaw, especially between the two upper front teeth.

"David Letterman and Madonna show us that one can be rich and famous with a prominent **diastema**."

DOL (DOHL): *n.* from Latin *dolor* (pain): a unit of pain intensity, as when pain is rated in severity from one to ten.

"Although using **dols** as estimates of pain is subjective, hospitals and other medical institutions use something like those measurements when they ask patients to rate pain from one to ten."

DYSCALCULIA (DIS-kow-**KYOO**-lee-uh): *n.* impairment of mathematical ability due to an organic condition of the brain.

"Gretchen's difficulty with math was not a product of bad study habits but **dyscalculia**, stemming from her brain."

DYSCHEZIA (dis-KEE-zee-uh): *n.* the inability to defecate without pain and difficulty.

"Carmen's **dyschezia** was a consequence of her habitually suppressing the urge to defecate at work."

DYSURIA (dis-YOOR-ee-uh): painful or difficult urination.

"Because of Tom's urinary tract infection, he had **dysuria**, which included a burning sensation."

ENCOPRESIS (EN-kuh-**PREE**-suhs): *n.* from Greek *kopros* (dung): involuntary defecation, especially in children who have usually already been toilet trained.

"To treat **encopresis** in children, many pediatricians recommend using stool softeners and scheduling toilet-sitting times (typically after meals)."

EXPLODING HEAD SYNDROME: *n.* a condition in which the sufferer sometimes experiences a tremendously loud noise as originating within his or her head, usually described as the sound of an explosion, a roar, a ringing, a buzzing, or even loud voices or screams.

"Those with **exploding head syndrome** usually experience it within an hour or two after falling asleep, though it isn't necessarily a result of a dream and can occur during wakefulness."

FESTINATING GAIT: *n.* from Latin *festinare* (to hasten): a style of walking in which a person involuntarily moves with short, accelerating steps, often on tiptoe, while the trunk is flexed forward, and the legs are flexed stiffly at the hips and knees.

"The man with a **festinating gait** had Parkinson's disease."

FORMICATION: *n.* from *formicare* (to crawl like an ant), from *formica* (ant): an abnormal sensation resembling the sensation made by insects (such as ants) creeping in or on the skin.

"**Formication**, which can be caused by diabetic neuropathy, skin cancer, herpes zoster, and other conditions, can trigger the scratch reflex and lead to skin damage from excessive scratching."

GLEET: *n.* from Middle English *glet* (slime), from Middle French *glete*, from Latin *glittus* (sticky): (i) a chronic inflammation of a bodily orifice in people or animals usually accompanied by an abnormal discharge from the orifice (nasal *gleet*); (ii) the discharge itself (as in the urethral mucous discharge in gonorrhea).

"Because of Mike's pain on urinating and thick, copious urethral **gleet**, he went to the doctor, fearing gonorrhea."

IATGROGENIC (EYE-a-troh-JEN-ik): *n.* from Greek *iatros* (physician) and *-genic* (produced by): induced by a physician, as by treatment, diagnosis, or suggestion.

"Sadly, even competent physicians can misdiagnose conditions and then mistreat patients, giving them **iatrogenic** diseases."

IDIOPATHIC (id-ee-uh-PATH-ik): *adj.* from New Latin *idiopathia* (primary disease), from Greek *idiopatheia* (feeling for oneself alone), from *idios* (personal, peculiar) and *-patheia*, from *paschein* (to expense, suffer): (i) peculiar to an individual; (ii) of diseases, arising from an obscure or unknown cause.

"When the doctor told Marty that his disease was **idiopathic**, Marty said, 'At least you know what we're dealing with.'"

KINETOSIS (KIN-uh-**TOH**-suhs): *n.* from Greek *kin-*, *kinēma* (motion) and *-ōsis* (disease caused by): motion sickness.

"Just getting up in the morning gives me **kinetosis**."

LIPOTHYMIC (LY-puh-**THIM**-ik): *adj.* (i) tending to swoon; (ii) fainting.

"Like many **lipothymic** Victorian literary heroines, Jane had trouble remaining conscious when she was excited."

LYSIS (LY-suhs): from Greek *lysis* (act of loosening or dissolving): the gradual lowering of a fever.

"After some aspirin and rest, the patient experienced **lysis**."

NYCTALOPIA (NIK-tuh-**LOH**-pee-uh): *n.* from Latin *nyctalops* (unable to see at twilight), from Greek *nyktalōp-*, *nyktalōps*, from *nykt* (night) and *alaos* (blind): (i) night-blindness; (ii) reduced vision in dim light or darkness.

"Because of my uncle's **nyctalopia**, he rarely drives at night."

OBDORMITION: *n.* from Latin *obdormire* (to fall asleep): the sensation of numbness that occurs in a limb when it "falls asleep" because of pressure on a nerve.

"Because I had slept on my right arm, I woke up experiencing **obdormition**."

PEDICULOUS: (pi-DI-kyuh-luhs): *adj.* infested with lice.

"Because Kenny was **pediculous**, he bought a pediculicide called Quell to get rid of the lice."

PHTHIRIASIS (thi-RY-uh-suhs, thy-RY-uh-suhs): *n.* from Greek *phtheiriasis*, from *phtheir* (louse) and -*iasis* (morbid state): infestation with crab lice (which attack the pubic area).

"When Roscoe said that he couldn't stand crabs, we didn't realize that he was talking about **phthiriasis**."

PURSY: *adj.* from Middle French *polsif*, from *polser* (to push, beat, breathe with difficulty): tending to be or habitually short-winded, especially because of corpulence.

"The **pursy** man was breathing heavily after he ran only ten yards."

PURULENT (PYOOR-uh-luhnt, PYOOR-yuh-luhnt): *n.* from Latin *purulentus* (festering): consisting of or being pus.

"Jordan used to soak his feet in hot water whenever his big toe with the ingrown toenail became infected and **purulent**."

PYGALGIA (py-GAL-jee-uh): *n.* from Greek *pyge* (rump, buttocks) and *algos* (pain): pain in the buttocks.

"Duke's **pygalgia** was due to his falling backward on a pile of stones.

RALE: *n.* from French *râle*, from *râler* (to make a rattling sound in the throat): now more commonly known as *crackles*, the clicking, rattling, or crackling noises heard when listening to the lungs with a stethoscope (*see* AUSCULTATION under "Medicine") during inhalation.

"**Rales** can be heard in patients with pneumonia, pulmonary fibrosis, acute bronchitis, and other diseases."

RHEUM (ROOM): *n.* from Greek *rheuma* (a flowing): thin mucus naturally discharged as a watery substance from the eyes, nose, or mouth, drying and gathering as a crust in the corners of the eyes (*see* LACRIMAL CARUNCLE under "Anatomy"), in the corners of the mouth, on the eyelids, or under the nose.

"Because people blink very little during sleep, **rheum** ('sleep' or 'sand') will often form in the corners of their eyes."

TENESMUS (tuh-NEZ-muhs): *n.* from Greek *teinesmos*, from *teinein* (to stretch, strain): a painful and distressing but ineffectual urge to evacuate the rectum or urinary bladder.

"Wilbur's visit to the bathroom was frustrating because of his **tenesmus**, which was not helped even with laxatives."

TERATOLOGY (TER-uh-**TOL**-uh-jee): *n.* from Greek *terat-*, *teras* (marvel, portent, monster): the study of malformations and other defects in births.

"Scholars who specialize in **teratology** can often predict the probability of many birth defects."

TIQUEUR (ti-KUR): *n.* from French *tiquer* (to have a tic, to twitch): a person affected with a tic.

"The man who interviewed me was a **tiqueur** whose facial movements distracted me."

TRENDELENBURG POSITION: *n.* a position in which the body is laid flat on the back (supine) with the feet higher than the head.

"The **Trendelenburg position**, which used to be the standard first aid position for shock, is still used at times in childbirth when a woman's cervix is too swollen and won't dilate to ten centimeters; it is also helpful in surgery for an abdominal hernia."

VALETUDINARIAN (VAL-uh-T(Y)OO-di-NAIR-ee-in): *n.* from Latin *valetudinarius* (sickly, infirm): a weak or sickly person, especially one morbidly concerned with one's invalidism.

"All the **valetudinarian** wanted to talk about was his illness."

~~~~~~

Medicine

~~~~~~

ANTITUSSIVE (an-TEE-TUS-iv, an-TY-TUS-iv): *adj.* from Greek *anti-* (opposite) and Latin *tussis* (cough): capable of relieving or suppressing coughing.

"When the holistic physician discovered my cough, she recommended licorice herbal tea for its **antitussive** property."

AUSCULTATION (AW-skuhl-**TAY**-shuhn): *n.* from Latin *auscultare* (to listen): the act of listening to sounds arising within organs (such as the lungs or heart) with a stethoscope or direct application of the ear to the body.

"Bill Cosby used to joke that, before physicians engage in **auscultation**, they keep their stethoscopes in refrigerators."

BABINSKI REFLEX: *n.* from Joseph *Babinski*, a French neurologist: the rising of the big toe and fanning of the small toes when the sole of the foot is stroked firmly on the outer side from the heel to the front.

"Although the **Babinski reflex** is normal in infants under two, it can be a sign of brain or spinal cord injury in older persons."

DÉBRIDEMENT (DAY-breed-**MAHN**, di-**BREED**-muhnt): *n.* from French *débridement*, from *débrider* (to unbridle): (i) medical removal of dead, devitalized, or contaminated tissue from a wound; (ii) in dentistry, removal of dental plaque and calculus.

"**Débridement** of wounds can be done in many ways, including surgery, the use of chemicals, and even the use of certain species of maggots that selectively eat necrotic tissue."

DICK TEST: *n.* from George *Dick* and Gladys *Dick* (American bacteriologists who worked on the diagnosis and treatment of scarlet fever in the 1920s): a skin test used to determine immunity or susceptibility to scarlet fever.

"Before antibiotics became widely used, people would commonly receive a **Dick test** to determine whether they were immune to scarlet fever."

MYDRIATIC (MID-ree-**AT**-ik): *adj.* from Greek *mydriasis* (prolonged dilation of the pupil of the eye): causing dilation of the pupils.

"When the nurse gave me **mydriatic** eye drops, I knew I'd need a green plastic insert for my glasses to protect my eyes from the bright sunlight as I drove home."

NOSOCOMIAL (NOHS-uh-**KOH**-mee-uhl): *adj.* from Greek *nosokomos* (person who tends the sick): originating or taking place in a hospital.

"A catheter was implicated in a **nosocomial** infection."

NOSOLOGY (noh-SAHL-uh-jee, noh-ZAHL-uh-jee): *n.* from Greek *nosos* (disease): a branch of medical science dealing with classifying diseases.

"A chief difficulty in **nosology** is that some diseases cannot be clearly defined and classified, especially when the causes are unknown."

OTOSCOPE (**OHD**-uh-SKOHP): *n.* from Greek *ōt-*, *ous* (ear) and *skopein* (to see): an instrument with lighting and a magnifying lens to inspect the auditory canal and eardrum.

"The doctor noticed a good deal of wax (*see* CERUMEN under "Bodily Products / Effects / Functions") when he examined Doris's ears with the **otoscope**."

PALPATION: *n.* from Latin *palpare* (to touch gently): in medicine, a physical examination in diagnosis by pressure of the hand or fingers to the surface of the body to determine the condition (as of size or consistency) of an underlying part or organ.

"The doctor's **palpation** of the woman's neck was to determine whether there was much swelling of the cervical lymph nodes."

PARVULE (PAHR-vyool): *n.* a very small pill.

"The brightly colored cylindrical **parvule** turned out to be LSD (orange barrel acid)."

PLEXOR (PLEK-suhr): *n.* from Greek *plēxis* (stroke): a small, rubber-headed hammer used in medical examination and diagnosis.

"The physician tapped my right knee with a **plexor**."

THALASSOTHERAPY: *n.* from Greek *thalassa* (sea) and English *therapy*: exposure to seawater (as in a hot tub) or application of seaweed or sea salt or other sea products to the body for health or beauty.

"Many people pay a great deal of money to visit resorts where they can receive **thalassotherapy**, as when people bathe in certain waters."

Meteorology

GRAUPEL (GROW-puhl): *n.* granular snow pellets.

"When supercooled droplets of water condense on a snowflake, the precipitation that forms is called *soft hail*, *snow pellets*, or **graupel**."

NEPHELOGNOSY (NEF-uh-**LAHG**-nuh-see): *n.* from Greek *nephos* (cloud) and *-gnosy* (knowledge): scientific observation of clouds.

"When Charlie got into a car accident because his eyes were on the clouds and not on the road, he tried to justify himself by saying that he was engaged in **nephelognosy**."

NEPHOMETER (ne-FAHM-i-tuhr): *n.* from Greek *nephos* (cloud) and English *-meter*: an instrument for measuring the amount of cloud cover in the sky.

"Most people don't need a **nephometer** to know how cloudy or sunny it is."

NEPHOSCOPE (NEF-uh-SKOHP): *n.* an instrument for observing the direction of motion and velocity of clouds.

"**Nephoscopes** can determine the direction of a cloud's motion by using radio waves."

SEREIN (suh-RAN): *n.* from Middle French *serain* (evening), from Latin *serum* (evening), from *serus* (late): in the tropics, a very fine rain that falls from a clear sky at dusk.

"In the evening, we enjoyed the **serein**, which fell from a clear sky a few moments after sunset."

SUBBOREAL: *adj.* from Latin *sub-* (under, below) and Greek *Boreas* (Greek god of the north wind): very cold though not quite freezing.

"It was thirty-five degrees Fahrenheit, a stimulating, **subboreal** temperature."

MILITARY

ANABASIS (uh-NAB-uh-suhs): *n.* from Greek *anabainein* (to go up, to go up from the coast): a military advance.

"The Russian **anabasis** caused Napoleon to retreat."

CHEVRON (SHEV-ruhn): *n.* a V-shaped or inverted V-shaped line or stripe, especially one on the sleeve of a uniform indicating military rank or length of service; in heraldry, an inverted *V.*

"A corporal E4 in the U.S. Army wears a double **chevron**."

DEBOUCH (di-BOWCH): *v.* from Latin *bucca* (puffed out cheek): in military usage, to march out into open ground.

"The soldiers were nervous as they **debouched** from the fort and moved toward enemy territory."

ENFILADE (EN-fuh-**LAYD**, EN-fuh-**LAHD**): *n.* sweeping gunfire across the length of a line of troops.

"When the soldiers tried to get out of their foxholes, they were exposed to an **enfilade** from the enemy."

ESCALATION AGILITY: *n.* in military language, the ease with which one side or the other can escalate in a weapons exchange.

"During the Cold War, the **escalation agility** of both the former Soviet Union and the United States deterred both sides from using nuclear weapons."

QUAKER GUN: *n.* in military tactics, a wooden log, usually painted black, to resemble an actual cannon, placed to mislead the enemy's estimation of one's strength.

"A **quaker gun** was famously used by American Colonel William Washington during the American Revolutionary War at the Battle of Rugeley's Mill, causing Loyalist Colonel Rowland Rugeley and his company to surrender without a shot being fired."

MONEY / PROPERTY

ENGRAILMENT: *n.* a ring of raised dots around the edge of a coin or medal.

"My uncle had within his coin collection silver coins with **engrailments**."

GAZUMP (guh-ZUHMP): *v.* in British real estate, to demand a higher price from the buyer of a house than that agreed on.

"When a Londoner raised the price of a house after a deal had been made, the buyer knew she had been **gazumped**."

HANDSEL (HAND-suhl): *n.* (i) a gift to express good wishes at the beginning of a new year or enterprise; (ii) the first money taken in by a new business or on the opening day, especially when considered a token of good luck.

"The merchant treated his first dollar as a **handsel** and had it framed."

NUMMIFORM (NUHM-uh-FORM): *adj.* from French *nummiforme*, from Latin *nummus* (coin): coin-shaped.

"At the restaurant, I ordered some **nummiform** fried potatoes."

ONIOMANIA (OH-nee-uh-**MAY**-nee-uh): *n.* from Greek *ōnios* (to be bought, for sale), from *ōnos* (price) and English *mania* (madness, frenzy): an uncontrollable urge to buy things.

"Because Nick's son, Steve, was known for **omniomania**, Nick made sure that Steve never had Nick's credit card."

RACK RATE: *n.* motel equivalent of "list price," the officially stated price of a room from which discounts are made.

"Because I have an AAA card and I wanted to stay at a motel during the off-season, my rate was much lower than the **rack rate**."

ROULEAU (roo-**LOO**): *n.* from Middle French *rolel*, diminutive of *role* (roll): a roll of coins put in paper.

"I went to the bank to get a **rouleau** of quarters."

SALARIAT: *n.* probably from analogy with *proletariat*: body of salaried persons, especially as distinguished from wage earners.

"Once Marvin left sales and became a full-time teacher, he became a member of the **salariat**."

SCORCHED-EARTH DEFENSE: *n.* from the name of a military strategy in which one destroys anything useful to one's enemy: in investing, an antitakeover strategy in which a target firm acts to make itself unattractive to the hostile bidder, as when a firm agrees to liquidate or destroy all valuable assets (*crown jewels*) or schedules debt repayment to be due immediately following a hostile takeover.

"A **scorched-earth defense** will almost certainly penalize the shareholders of the target firm."

VIATICUM (vy-AT-i-kum): *n.* an allowance (as of transportation, supplies, and money) for traveling.

"Because of my company's generous **viaticum**, I was able to stay at an excellent hotel."

MORALITY

ADIAPHOROUS (AD-ee-**AF**-uh-ruhs): *adj.* from Greek *adiaphoros*, from *a-* (not) and *diaphoros* (different): (i) morally neutral or indifferent; (ii) in medicine, neither helpful nor harmful.

"The theologian asserted that although eating vegetables is **adiaphorous**, eating people is immoral."

EXIGIBLE (EK-suh-juh-buhl): *adj.* from French *exiger* (to demand): that may be exacted or required, as a duty.

"The drill sergeant told his daughter that making her bed was not optional but **exigible**."

SUPEREROGATORY (SOO-puhr-i-**RAH**-guh-TOR-ee): *adj.* from Latin *supererogare* (to pay in addition): observed or performed beyond the call of duty.

"When firefighters risk their lives to save others, they

are admirably doing their duty; when ordinary people risk their lives to save complete strangers, they are probably doing what is **supererogatory**."

MUSIC / MUSICAL INSTRUMENTS / MUSICIANS

CAMPANOLOGIST: *n.* from Latin *campana* (bell): one skilled at bell ringing.

"Years ago during variety TV shows, such as *The Ed Sullivan Show*, some **campanologist** would play songs by using several different bells lying atop a table."

CAPOTASTO (KAP-poh-TA-STOH): *n.* from Italian *cap* (head) and *tasto* (tie, fret): a bar or movable nut attached to a guitar, mandolin, or banjo to raise the pitch of all the strings.

"By using a **capotasto** (capo), a musician needn't learn a song in several different keys if accompanying singers sing in different pitches."

CHANTER: *n.* from Latin *cantare* (to sing): the reed pipe of a bagpipe with finger holes on which the melody is played.

"The **chanter** on the bagpipe looked like a flute, though it was attached to a bag rather than someone's mouth."

CHEVALET (shuh-VA-lay, SHEV-uh-LAY): *n.* from French, diminutive of *cheval* (horse): the bridge of a stringed musical instrument.

"When Debbie tossed the uncased violin on the backseat of the car, she broke the **chevalet**."

C-HOLE: *n.* a *C*-shaped sound hole, as in viols.

"When Bob asked Jeff to let Bob see Jeff's viol, Jeff said, 'No A-hole will touch my **C-hole**.'"

F-HOLE: *n.* a long, narrow hole in the soundboard (or top surface) of a violin that looks like an old-fashioned *f* or *S* to modern eyes.

"Violins have two **f-holes**, one on each side of the bridge."

NONET (noh-NET): *n.* from Italian *nonetto*, from diminutive of *nono* (ninth), from Latin *nonus* (ninth): (i) a combination of nine instruments or voices; (ii) a composition written for such a combination.

"Because we had nine musicians, we performed one of Johannes Brahms's serenades designed for a **nonet**."

NOODLING: *n.* music that is played as titles or credits roll.

"I didn't leave until after the credits because I enjoyed listening to the **noodling**."

PARADIDDLE (par-uh-DID-uhl): *n.* probably of onomatopoeic origin: a basic drumroll.

"An excellent drummer will be quite capable of a **paradiddle**."

ZILL: *n.* probably from Turkish *zil* (bell, cymbals): a small metallic cymbal used in pairs, with one worn on the thumb and the other worn on the middle finger.

"The belly dancer's **zills** were made of brass."

OCCUPATIONS

COOPER: *n.* one who makes or repairs barrels.

"The merchant gave the broken wooden cask to a **cooper** for repair."

DOGBERRY: *n.* from *Dogberry*, a foolish constable in Shakespeare's *Much Ado about Nothing*: a blundering official, often a police officer or constable.

"In the *Police Academy* movies, almost every police officer was depicted as a **Dogberry**."

EPIGONE (EP-i-GOHN): *n.* from Greek *epigonos* (one born after): an inferior imitator of a distinguished creative person (artist, musician, philosopher, etc.).

"The most successful radio talk show host of all time wasn't worried by competitors, consisting mostly of **epigones**."

FACTOTUM: *n.* from Latin *facere* (to do, make) and *totum* (everything): a worker who serves in a wide range of capacities.

"The employee doesn't have one overarching responsibility but is a **factotum**."

FAGIN (FAY-guhn): *n.* from *Fagin*, a fence and trainer of children as pickpockets in Charles Dickens's novel *Oliver Twist*: an adult who instructs children in crime (especially theft).

"The man was a **fagin** who used adolescent thieves to run his stolen goods."

FOOTPAD: *n.* from English *foot* and obsolete *pad* (highwayman): a thief who robs pedestrians.

"When the English professor was asked whether the robbers left in a car, he replied that they were **footpads**."

GAFFOON: *n.* in TV broadcasting, a person responsible for sound effects.

"We asked the **gaffoon** on the TV set to create the sound of hiccups."

LOBSTER SHIFT / TRICK: *n.* a work shift (as on a newspaper) that covers the late evening and early morning hours.

"On the newspaper those working the **lobster shift** (or **lobster trick**) are part of a reduced staff."

LYCHNOBITE (LIK-nuh-byt): *n.* from Greek *lychnos* (lamp) and *bios* (life): one who works at night and sleeps in the day.

"Some **lychnobites** either put aluminum foil on their bedroom windows or use heavy curtains so that they can more easily sleep during the day."

PINK COLLAR: *adj.* pertaining to jobs, such as those of elementary-school teachers, telephone operators, and secretaries, traditionally held by women.

"The economist acknowledged that certain U.S. jobs are still **pink-collar** jobs (including the job of dental hygienists), but he denied that women nowadays are forced into lower-paying jobs because of their sex."

TILLERMAN: *n.* one who steers the rear wheels of a fire engine or controls its ladder.

"Jack was a **tillerman** whose skill in manipulating the rear wheels of a fire truck allowed the truck to turn onto narrow streets."

~~~~~~

Ornaments

~~~~~~

LABRET (LAY-bruht): *n.* from Latin *labrum* (lip): an ornament worn in a perforation of the lip.

"The dentist felt uncomfortable when his hygienist began wearing a **labret** in her lip."

NEF: *n.* from French *nef* (nave, boat-shaped vessel): (i) a sixteenth-century clock in the form of a ship having mechanical devices to illustrate astronomical movements; (ii) an ornamental table utensil used for holding a napkin, knife, and spoon and shaped like a ship.

"The former sailor had a **nef** on the dinner table that held eating utensils."

PHILOSOPHY

AGATHIST (AG-uh-thist): *n*. from Greek *agathos* (good): a person who believes that all things tend toward ultimate good.

"The self-made millionaire was an **agathist**, believing that our setbacks contain the seeds of a compensatory benefit."

HETERONOMOUS: *adj*. (i) originating outside the self or one's own will; (ii) subject to external controls and impositions.

"For Immanuel Kant, a good will—the desire to do what is right because it is right—originates within the self and is never **heteronomous**."

MALISM (MAY-liz-uhm): *n*. from Latin *malus* (bad): the doctrine that the world is evil.

"The German philosopher Arthur Schopenhauer's **malism** led him to write that it is a sin to be born and that to desire immortality is to desire the eternal perpetuation of a great mistake."

MELIORISM (MEEL-yuh-RIZ-uhm): *n*. from Latin *melior* (better): the doctrine that the world tends to become better and that humanity has the power to improve it.

"**Meliorism** is intimately connected with a belief in

progress, in the ability of human beings to improve conditions through their intervention in processes that would otherwise be natural."

MONOGENISM (muh-**NAHJ**-uh-NIZ-uhm): *n.* from Greek *monos* (one) and combining form *-gen* (be born, causing, producing): the belief that the human race is descended from two persons, such as Adam and Eve.

"The preacher told his congregation that he believed in **monogenism** and in the historical reality of Adam and Eve."

PHILOSOPHASTER (fi-**LAHS**-uh-FAS-tur): *n.* from Latin *philosophus* (philosopher) and *-aster* (a diminutive suffix with derogatory implication): a pretender or dabbler in philosophy.

"The evangelist called the agnostic philosopher 'an arrogant **philosophaster**.'"

PSEUDODOX (**SOU**-duh-DAHKS): *n.* from Greek *pseudodoxos* (holding a false opinion), from *pseudodoxein* (to hold a false opinion): a false opinion or doctrine.

"When people hold a **pseudodox**, they normally think that their belief is true."

QUODLIBET (**KWAHD**-li-bet): *n.* from Latin *quod libet* (what you will, as you please): (i) a subtle or debatable point, especially a theological or scholastic question proposed for argument or disputation; (ii) a scholastic or theological debate over a highly subtle point.

"Someone who discusses theological **quodlibets** in the philosophy of Alfred North Whitehead is capable of understanding things in which billions of people are not the least interested."

TRILEMMA (tri-LEM-uh): *n.* a situation offering three difficult options.

"C. S. Lewis once wrote that people have a **trilemma** if they accept the historical existence of Jesus: people must, according to Lewis, think that he was who, according to the Bible, he claimed to be, or a liar, or a madman."

VERIDICAL (vuh-RID-i-kuh): *adj.* from *veridicus* (veracious), from *verus* (true) and *dicere* (to say): (i) truthful, veracious; (ii) not illusory but genuine, real, actual.

"A major goal in Descartes's philosophy was to find indubitable methods for distinguishing **veridical** experience from illusory experience."

PLUMBING

BIBCOCK: *n.* a faucet with a bent-down nozzle; also known as a *bib* or *bibb*.

"Outside faucets for gardening are usually **bibcocks**."

BUBBLER: *n.* (i) the metal part of a drinking fountain out of which water comes; (ii) the fountain itself.

"The water squirted from the **bubbler** with such pressure that the boy who drank from it became wet."

DIVERTER: *n.* a valve, as in a bathtub, used to change the flow of fluid through a system of pipes.

"Bobby pulled out the **diverter** in the bathtub to take a shower."

PETCOCK: *n.* a small cock, faucet, or valve to control the flow of liquid or gas.

"Most older motorcycles have a fuel **petcock** either on or near the fuel tank to control the supply of gasoline."

POLITICS

EPURATION (ep-yuh-RAY-shun): *n.* from French *épurer* (to purify, purge): purification, especially the removal of officials or politicians considered disloyal.

"The conservative social critic called for the **epuration** of moderate Republican politicians in the upcoming elections."

LOGROLLING: *n.* the trading of votes by legislators to secure favorable action on projects of interest to one another.

"Politically, **logrolling** is a form of back scratching by which politicians supply pork to their constituents by helping other politicians supply pork to theirs."

PSEPHOLOGY (see-FAHL-uh-jee): *n.* from Greek *psēphos* (ballot, pebble): the study and statistical analysis of political elections.

"The political scientist I met, a specialist in recognizing current voting patterns and predicting future ones, is a leading expert in **psephology**."

ROORBACK (ROOR-bak): *n.* from Baron Von *Roorback*, fictional author of *Roorback's Tour Through the Western and Southern States*, an imaginary book from which an alleged passage was quoted in *Ithaca* (New York) *Chronicle* of 1844 that made scurrilous charges against James K. Polk, then Democratic candidate for the presidency: a defamatory falsehood published to harm someone politically, especially before an election.

"Both Democrats and Republicans have circulated **roorbacks** right before elections to attack politicians without giving them time to defend themselves."

PRINTING AND TYPESETTING

AGITRON: *n.* from "Beetle Bailey" cartoonist Mort Walker: wiggly lines in comic strips indicating that something is shaking.

"The cartoonist used **agitrons** to indicate that the water in a glass was shaking."

ASCENDER: *n.* in printing, the part of a lowercase letter that rises above the main body.

"The letters *b* and *t* have **ascenders**."

BREVE (BREEV, BREV): *n.* a small mark, like a tiny smile, placed over a vowel to represent the "short" sound of the vowel.

"The short sound of the *a* in *mat* could be represented with a **breve**—thus ă."

CEREMONIAL OPENING: *n.* the beginning of a book chapter with a large ornamental letter.

"The book began with the word *Once*, whose first letter was ornamental to express a **ceremonial opening**."

CIRCUS MAKEUP: *n.* the use of many different typefaces to create attention.

"The **circus makeup** on the sign for the estate sale attracted the attention of many people."

COLOPHON (KAHL-uh-fuhn): *n.* from Greek *kolophōn* (summit, finishing touch): a publisher's identifying mark or emblem on the title page of a book.

"The publisher's **colophon** was an image of an owl."

DESCENDER: *n.* in printing, the part of a letter that falls below the main text body, as in *p*, *q*, and *y*.

"The word *buddy* has only one **descender**, which appears on the letter *y*."

FISTNOTE: *n.* a usually important note (as in a book) preceded by a printing character in the shape of a fist with pointed index finger.

"The **fistnote** in the textbook expressed an important distinction to help readers understand the previous discussion."

FLEURON (FLUHR-uhn): from Middle French *floron*, from *flor*, *flour*, *flur* (flower): a stylized flower used in printing, as on borders of stationery or on wedding invitations.

"Natalie, who loved flowers, had stationery with **fleurons** in the borders."

GRAWLIX: *n.* from "Beetle Bailey" cartoonist Mort Walker: a string of typographical symbols, such as @#$%&!, to represent an obscenity or a swearword.

"If the cartoonist had used swearwords instead of a **grawlix**, his cartoon wouldn't have been syndicated in hundreds of newspapers."

INCUNABULA: *n. pl.* from Latin *incunabula* (swaddling clothes, cradle, virgin, birthplace): books printed before 1501.

"The **incunabula** were housed in a special section of the library to which there was restricted access."

LEADERS: *n. pl.* in printing, a line of dots, such as those used in the contents and indexes of books.

"The **leaders** in a table of contents lead the reader's eyes from the name of each chapter to a page number."

MACRON (MAY-krahn): *n.* from Greek *makros* (long): a mark place over a vowel to indicate that the pronunciation is long.

"The *a* in the word *sane* could have a **macron** over it when illustrating its pronunciation—thus ā."

OCTOTHORPE (AHK-tuh-THORP): *n.* origin uncertain: the pound sign (#).

"The operator asked me to press a number and then the **octothorpe** on the touch pad."

OPTOTYPE: *n.* specially shaped letters, numbers, or geometric symbols used to test visual acuity, as on an eye chart.

"On many eye charts the first three rows of **optotypes** are, respectively, *E*, *FP*, and *TOZ*."

PECULIARS: *n. pl.* in British printing, special characters not generally included in standard type fonts, such as phonetic symbols and mathematical symbols.

"The typist went online to find some **peculiars**, including phonetic symbols."

SCREAMER: *n.* in newspapers, a very large banner headline set in bold print.

"When a sitting U.S. president dies, we expect to see a **screamer** in the newspaper."

SECOND COMING TYPE: *n.* the largest, boldest headline type available to a newspaper.

"Newspapers will use **second coming type** when some extraordinarily gripping event occurs, such as the horror of September 11, 2001, or the great achievement of the first moonwalk in 1969."

SINKAGE: *n.* the distance from the top line of a full page to the first line of lowered matter.

"Because chapter titles are lower than most other type, the **sinkage** on pages of chapter titles must be adjusted."

SLUG: *n.* in newspaper or magazine writing, a very brief identifying headline used at the top of the continued portion of an article.

"The **slug** for an article headlined 'Administration Supports Massive Bailout' might simply say 'Bailout.'"

TAILPIECE: *n.* a small ornament or illustration at the end of a book chapter or magazine article.

"At the end of the article in the bodybuilding magazine was a **tailpiece** in the form of a dumbbell."

VERSO: *n.* from New Latin *verso* (folio), the page being turned: left-hand page (as of a book).

"A **verso** of a book usually carries an even page number."

PSYCHIATRY

ANALYSAND (uh-NAL-uh-sand): *n.* from *analyze* and *-and* (as in multiplicand): one who is receiving psychoanalysis.

"Woody told us that he is not a psychiatric patient but rather an **analysand**."

ANHEDONIA (AN-hee-**DOH**-nee-uh): *n.* from Greek *an-* (without) and *hēdonē* (pleasure): the inability to experience pleasure or happiness. By the way, *Anhedonia* was the original title of Woody Allen's film *Annie Hall*, but United Artists rejected it.

"Larry David, in the TV show *Curb Your Enthusiasm*, like Woody Allen in most of his movies, plays a character who constantly complains and whose **anhedonia** is a running joke."

CACOËTHES (KAK-oh-EE-theez): *n.* from Greek *kakoēthes* (wickedness), from neuter of *kakoēthēs* (malignant), from *kak-*, *cac-* and *-ēthēs*, from *ēthos* (custom): (i) a habitual and uncontrollable desire; (ii) mania.

"Although some may envy the sexual 'conquests' of President Clinton and Tiger Woods, most people, including nearly all women, find sexual **cacoëthes** and serial adultery repellent."

CAPGRAS DELUSION: *n.* from Joseph *Capgras*, a French psychiatrist: a disorder in which people hold a delusion that a friend, spouse, or parent or other close family member has been replaced by an identical-looking impostor.

"The psychiatrist said that either the film *The Invasion of the Body Snatchers* describes possibly real events or one of his patients has the **Capgras delusion**."

CARPHOLOGY: *n.* from Greek *karphologia*, from *karphos* (twig, straw, piece of wood) and *-logia* (collection): aimless and semiconscious plucking at bedclothes observed in those suffering exhaustion, stupor, or high fever.

"Had Roberta not had a high fever, her **carphology** would have shocked us."

COTARD'S SYNDROME: *n.* from French neurologist Jules *Cotard*: also known as *nihilistic* or *negation delusion*, a rare neuropsychiatric disorder in which people believe that they are dead (either figuratively or literally), don't exist, are putrefying, or have lost their blood or internal organs.

"Anyone who sincerely tells you that he is dead may have **Cotard's syndrome**."

EMPLEOMANIA (EM-plee-oh-**MAY**-nee-uh): *n.* a mania for holding public office.

"Anyone who runs unsuccessfully for office three or more times must have **empleomania**."

JERUSALEM SYDROME: *n.* a group of mental phenomena involving religiously themed obsessive ideas, delusions, or psychosis-like experiences that are triggered by, or lead to, a visit to Jerusalem.

"Although some psychiatrists submit that people with no psychiatric problems have spontaneously suffered from the **Jerusalem syndrome**, other psychiatrists assert that nearly all those suffering from the syndrome have displayed psychiatric problems before the trip to Jerusalem."

WORD SALAD: *n.* a jumble of incoherent speech, a common symptom of advanced schizophrenia.

"Although some schizophrenics are verbally adroit and even creative, others utter **word salads** that defy listeners' comprehension."

PSYCHOLOGY

ABULIA (uh-B(Y)OO-lee-uh): *n.* from Greek *a-* (without, not) and *boulē* (will): loss or lack of will or motivation, usually expressed by an inability to make decisions or to set goals.

"Danny's **abulia** was so pronounced that he constantly had trouble deciding what he wanted to eat."

CONFABULATE: *v.* in psychology, to fill in gaps in one's memory with fabrications that one believes to be factual.

"Not all false statements are lies; sometimes people **confabulate**, filling in memory gaps with plausible-sounding details that seem correct to the speaker or writer."

DESIRE LINE / PATH: *n.* from French philosopher Gaston Bachelard in his book *The Poetics of Space*: a path developed by erosion caused by animal or human walking, as when people create a path by taking the shortest or most easily navigated route between an origin and destination.

"Even before the advent of city planning, people used **desire lines** produced by animals to navigate from one location to another."

GROK (GRAHK): *v.* from Robert A. Heinlein's *Stranger in a Strange Land* (1961): (i) to understand especially profoundly and intuitively; (ii) to establish a deep compassionate rapport with.

"The politician, when caught with a call girl, insisted that his interests weren't purely carnal; rather, he claimed that he understood her to the point of **grokking** her in her fullness."

LAW OF EXERCISE: *n.* the principle that repetition of an act promotes learning and makes later performance of the act easier, other things being equal.

"When Olympic athletes or concert pianists practice eight hours a day, they are taking advantage of the **law of exercise**."

LAW OF RECENCY: *n.* the generalization holding that things most recently learned are best remembered.

"The **law of recency** implies that it will be easier to recall a new telephone number dialed a few minutes ago than to recall the same number dialed last week."

LUDIC: *adj.* from Latin *ludus* (play): of, relating to, or characterized by, undirected spontaneous playfulness.

"The scientist held that play reflects genetically ingrained **ludic impulses**, which can achieve full expression only in certain environments."

PAREIDOLIA (payr-EYE-DOHL-ee-uh): *n.* from *para* (beside) and *eidolon* (image): the subjective seeing or recognizing of patterns or connections in random or meaningless data (as in images or sounds), as when people claim to see a face on the surface of Mars, a face in clouds, or the face of an important religious figure formed on a mundane object, such as a piece of toast.

"A good example of **pareidolia** occurred in 1978, when

a New Mexican woman claimed to have found in the burn marks on a tortilla she had made Jesus Christ's face, prompting thousands of people to see the framed tortilla."

PRISONER'S CINEMA: *n.* a phenomenon reported by prisoners confined to dark cells or by others kept in darkness for a long time, consisting of a "light show" of various colors that appear out of the darkness, sometimes resolving into human or other figures.

"Many scientists think that the **prisoner's cinema** is a result of internally caused images combined with the psychological effects of prolonged exposure to darkness."

SUBAUDITION: *n.* the act of understanding or supplying something not expressed.

"We needed to be explicit in our instruction because some of the workers weren't good at **subaudition**."

VELLEITY (ve-LEE-i-tee, vuh-LEE-i-tee): *n.* from New Latin *velleitas*, from Latin *velle* (to wish): a slight wish, without any desire to expend energy to fulfill it.

"New Year's resolutions are often mere **velleities** because people are unwilling to pay the price for achieving them."

ZEIGARNIK EFFECT: *n.* from Bluma *Zeigarnik*, a twentieth-century German psychiatrist: the tendency to remember unfinished business and to forget finished business.

"Because Nelson would rarely complete tasks he started, the **Zeigarnik effect** enabled him to remember all his nonachievements."

Punctuation Marks

BRACE: *n.* either of complementary punctuation marks ({ }) used to enclose textual material.

"**Braces** are used to group not only words but also mathematical expressions."

VIRGULE (VUR-gyool): *n.* from Latin *virgula* (small rod, small stripe), diminutive of *virga* (branch, rod, stripe): a diagonal punctuation mark (/) used to separate related items of information, as in "and/or," also known as a *separatrix* and a *slash*.

"Whenever you see the expression *and/or*, you are seeing a **virgule**."

PUNISHMENTS
(INCLUDING EXECUTIONS)

BILBO (BIL-boh): *n.* perhaps from *Bilboa*, Spain: a long iron bar with sliding shackles attached to the ankles of prisoners.

"**Bilboes** were often used to shackle prisoners who were put on ships."

GANCH: *v.* from Turkish *kancalamak* (to put on a hook): to execute people by dropping them from a high place upon sharp stakes or hooks.

"The Turks used to execute criminals by **ganching** them."

LAPIDATE (LAR-i-DAYT): *v.* from Latin *lapidatus*, past participle of *lapidare* (to stone): to stone to death.

"When men were preparing to **lapidate** a woman accused of adultery, Jesus told them that only those without sin should cast stones."

NOYADE (NWAH-yahd): *n.* from French *noyer* (to drown): execution by mass drowning, a mode of execution during the Reign of Terror in France toward the close of 1793 and the beginning of 1794.

"During the Reign of Terror, bound prisoners were put

on a ship with a movable bottom, which was opened, killing them by a **noyade**."

TALION (TAL-ee-uhn): from Latin *talio* (punishment in kind for injury sustained): (i) punishment that exacts a penalty corresponding in kind to the crime; (ii) retaliation.

"When the man called for the death penalty for murder, he held that **talion** represents justice because it proportions the punishment to the crime."

~~~~~~

RECEPTACLES

~~~~~~

CHIMB (CHYM): *n.* the rim of a barrel or a cask.

"When the barrel fell, part of its **chimb** on top was broken."

ETUI (ay-TWEE): an ornamental case for small articles (such as glasses, scissors, or needles) in daily use.

"The young woman kept her comb, scissors, and tweezers in an **etui**."

SNORKEL BOX: *n.* a mailbox with a protruding receiver to allow people to deposit mail without leaving their cars.

"Right before Christmas the **snorkel box** was so full that people could have snatched envelopes from the top of the box."

ULLAGE (UHL-ij): *n.* from Old French *euillier* (to fill up), from Latin *oculus* (eye), with reference to a container's bunghole: (i) the amount a container such as a wine bottle or cask falls short of being full; (ii) the amount of liquid within a container that has been lost, as through leakage, evaporation, or shipping.

"Because of an unusual leak, the **ullage** of the wine bottle was greater than expected."

RECREATIONAL LINGUISTICS

ALTERNADE: *n.* in recreational linguistics, a word that can be broken up into its odd-numbered and even-numbered letters (two sequences of every second letter) to form shorter words.

"The word *calliopes* is an **alternade** because it forms two other words when broken into its odd-numbered and even-numbered letters CaLlIoPeS and cAlLiOpEs (*clips* and *aloe*)."

ANTI-KANGAROO WORD: *n.* in recreational linguistics, a word that contains its antonym.

"The word *covert* is an **anti-kangaroo word** because it contains *overt*."

APOSTROPHE WORD: *n.* in recreational linguistics, a word with an apostrophe in it that becomes another word if the apostrophe is removed.

"The words *I'll*, *can't*, and *we'll* are all **apostrophe words** (*ill*, *cant*, and *well*)."

APTAGRAM: *n.* in recreational linguistics, a word that, when its letters are suitably rearranged, forms a word strongly related in meaning to the original word.

"The words *arise* and *raise* are apt anagrams or **aptagrams,** as are *evil* and *vile*."

APTRONYM: *n.* in recreational linguistics, a person's name that is particularly well suited to the person's profession.

"The former astronaut Sally Ride and former White House spokesperson Larry Speakes possessed **aptronyms**."

CAPITONYM: *n.* in recreational linguistics, a word whose pronunciation and meaning change when capitalized.

"Because the word *Polish* (pertaining to Poland) is pronounced differently from *polish* and has a different meaning, the words *Polish* and *polish* are **capitonyms,** as are *Tangier* and *tangier*, *August* and *august*, and *Nice* and *nice*."

CHARACTONYM: *n.* in recreational linguistics, a literary character's name that especially fits his or her personality.

"Charles Dickens was brilliant at creating **charactonyms,** as witness Mr. Gradagrind (tyrannical schoolmaster), Jaggers (a rough-edged lawyer), and Miss Havesham ("have a sham," a jilted spinster living an illusion)."

CHARADE: *n.* in recreational linguistics, a set of words formed by respacing but not rearranging the letters of another word, phrase, or sentence.

"The words *bedevil* (*bed* + *evil*), *Chicago* (*chic* + *ago*), and *pleasure* (*plea* + *sure*) are **charades**."

CONSONYM: *n.* in recreational linguistics, a word having the same consonants in the same order as another word.

"The words *eTHNiC* and *THeNCe* are **consonyms** of each other."

CONTRANYM: *n.* in recreational linguistics, a word with opposite or contrasting meanings, sometimes called a Janus-faced word, because of having two faces.

"Because *cleave* can mean 'to cut apart' and 'to seal together,' and because *buckle* can mean 'to hold together' and 'to collapse or fall apart,' *cleave* and *buckle* are **contranyms**."

DOMUNYM: *n.* in recreational linguistics, a word that identifies people from a particular place.

"The **domunym** for people from Norfolk, Virginia, is *Norfolkians*, whereas that for people from Norfolk, Nebraska, is *Norfolkans*."

GRAMMAGRAM: *n.* in recreational linguistics, a word that, when it is pronounced, sounds like a string of letters.

"**Grammagrams** are sometimes on personalized auto license plates, as in *QT* (cutey) and *DVS* (devious)."

HETERONYM: *n.* in recreational linguistics, a word with the same spelling as another word but with a different pronunciation and meaning.

"The word *minute* (MIN-it) as a measure of time is a **heteronym** because it can also be pronounced as my-NOOT, in which case it represents a measurement of size."

KANGAROO WORD: *n.* in recreational linguistics, a word that contains within itself another word that is a synonym of itself, as in *evacuate*, which contains *vacate*.

"Because the word *masculine* contains *male*, it is a **kangaroo word**."

LIPOGRAM: *n.* from Middle Greek *lipogrammatos* (lacking a letter): writing composed of words that don't have a certain letter, such as Tryphiodorus's *Odyssey*, which had no alpha in the first book, no beta in the second, and so on.

"Writing **lipograms** is simple for uncommon letters, such as *Z*, *J*, or *X*, but ingenuity is needed when **lipograms** omit the letters *A*, *E*, or *T* from large paragraphs."

PANGRAM: *n.* from Greek *pas*, *pantos* (all, the whole) and *gramma* (letter): a short sentence containing all twenty-six letters of the English alphabet.

"'The quick brown fox jumps over the lazy dog' is a famous English **pangram**."

PIANO WORD: *n.* in recreational linguistics, a word in which all its letters can be played as notes (a, b, c, d, e, f, g) on musical instruments.

"*Cabbage* and *bag* are examples of **piano words**."

SEMORDNILAP: *n.* from the word *palindromes* spelled in reverse: in recreational linguistics, a word, phrase, or sentence that, when its letters are reversed, spells another word, phrase, or sentence.

"The words *desserts* and *stressed* are **semordnilaps**."

TYPEWRITER WORD: *n.* in recreational linguistics, a word that can be typed on a single row of a typewriter, such as the words *typewriter*, *perpetuity*, *proprietor*, and *haggadahs*.

"When asked for a **typewriter word** beginning with *A*, the logophile immediately replied, *alfalfas*."

~~~~~~~~~~~~~~~~~~~~~~~~~~~~~~~~

RELIGION

~~~~~~~~~~~~~~~~~~~~~~~~~~~~~~~~

ACROAMATIC (**AK**-roh-uh-**MAD**-ik): *adj.* told orally to chosen disciples only.

"In Mark 4:11–12, Jesus distinguishes his parables, given for the uninitiated, from his **acroamatic** sayings, reserved only for his disciples."

ANTINOMIAN (AN-ti-**NOH**-mee-nhn): *n.* from Greek *anti-* (opposing, against) and *nomos* (law): in Christian theology, one who believes in the doctrine that, because of grace, right conduct is unnecessary for salvation.

"When the minister was asked how his scandalous adultery could be reconciled with his Christianity, he replied, 'I'm an **antinomian**.'"

APIKOROS (AP-ee-**KOR**-uhs): *n.* from Yiddish *apikurus*, from Hebrew *apīqōrōs*, from Greek *Epikouros* (Epicurus, humanistic Greek philosopher): a Jew who is lax in observing Jewish law or who doesn't believe in Judaism.

"Mort had a strong Jewish identity, but when it came to practicing Jewish law, he was an **apikoros**."

ASPERGE: *v.* from Latin *aspergere* (to sprinkle): to sprinkle with holy water.

"Members of the congregation felt cleansed after they were **asperged** by the priest."

ASPERGILLUM (**AS**-puhr-**JIL**-uhm): *n.* from Latin *aspergere* (to sprinkle): a brush or perforated container used by Roman Catholics for sprinkling holy water.

"After the acolyte poured some urine into the **aspergillum**, his days as an acolyte were numbered."

BULLA: *n.* from Latin *bulla* (bubble, boss, amulet): the round usually lead seal attached to papal bulls from the Roman Catholic pope who uses it.

"On one side of a **bulla** is a representation of St. Peter and St. Paul, and on the other side is the name of the pope who uses it."

COMMINATION (**KAHM**-uh-**NAY**-shuhn); *n.* from Latin *comminari* (to threaten): an instance of the action of announcing, warning of, or threatening punishment or vengeance, especially divine punishment.

"The minister's fiery sermons were represented as God's **comminations**, threatening sinners with punishment."

CONVENTICLE: *n.* from *conventus* (assembly): a secret or unlawful religious assembly, especially one conducted by those whose beliefs or practices run counter to those of the established church.

"Because of a fear of subversive sectarianism, **conventicles** were once condemned by mainstream Lutheranism."

CREDENCE TABLE: *n.* a small side table that is used to celebrate the Eucharist in the sanctuary of a Christian church.

"In a traditional Roman Catholic Mass, the chalice is placed on the **credence table** for the beginning of the service."

CROSIER (KROH-zhuhr): *n.* from Old High German *Krucka* (crutch): the ceremonial pastoral staff of a bishop, abbot, or abbess resembling a shepherd's crook and carried as a symbol of the pastoral office.

"Normally, a bishop will hold a **crosier** in the left hand, freeing the right hand to bestow blessings; the bishop or head of a church bears that staff as a 'shepherd of the flock of God.'"

DAVEN (DAH-vuhn): *v.* from Yiddish *davnen* (to pray): to recite Jewish prayers, usually with a back-and-forth swaying motion.

"The elderly man would sway back and forth as he would **daven** during Saturday morning prayer."

DULIA (doo-LY-uh): *n.* from Medieval Latin, from Late Greek *douleia* (service, work done, business), from Greek for "slavery," from *doulos* (slave): (i) in Roman Catholicism, veneration paid to saints and angels as servants and friends of God; (ii) veneration inferior to that given to the Virgin Mary (*see* HYPERDULIA).

"The Roman Catholic priest submitted that St. Paul deserves **dulia** because of his extraordinary role in promoting Christianity."

ESCHATOLOGY (es-kuh-TAH-luh-jee): *n.* from Greek *eschatos* (last, farthest): a branch of theology concerned with the final events in the history of the world or of humankind, often including beliefs and theories about death, judgment, heaven, and hell.

"The evangelist lamented Americans' declining interest in **eschatology** by saying that most Americans are more concerned about making ends meet than about meeting their end."

FIDEISM (**FY**-dee-**IZ**-uhm, **FEE**-day-**IZ**-uhm, **FI**-di-**IZ**-uhm): *n.* from Latin *fides* (faith): any doctrine according to which all or some religious knowledge depends on faith or revelation rather than reason.

"Both St. Paul and Martin Luther emphasized religious faith and promoted **fideism** while depreciating reason or philosophy, as when St. Paul asserted that worldly wisdom is folly to God, and Luther called reason a 'sweet whore.'"

FLABELLUM: *n.* from Latin *flabellum* (fan): in Roman Catholic liturgical use, a fan carried by attendants to the pope or a priest to keep flies from sacramental bread and wine.

"Because of the infestation of flies, the attendants had to use the **flabellum** more often than usual to protect the bread and wine."

HAGIOLATRY (**HAG**-ee-**AHL**-uh-tree, **HAY**-jee-**AHL**-uh-tree): *n.* the invocation or worship of saints.

"The young football player's esteem for his coach bordered on **hagiolatry**."

HAMARTIOLOGY (huh-**MAHR**-dee-**AH**-uh-jee): from Greek *hamartanein* (to err): a part of theology dealing with the doctrine of sin.

"After Mike held that sin doesn't admit of gradations,

Jake responded that any **hamartiology** that can't distinguish between getting drunk and committing genocide is too superficial to be worth discussing."

HERETICATE: *v.* to pronounce or denounce as heretical—that is, contrary to accepted beliefs or standards.

"Pelagianism, which rejected original sin and which embraced the belief that people can choose not to sin, was **hereticated** during the fifth century CE."

HOMILETIC (HAHM-uh-LET-ik): *adj.* from Greek *homilein* (to consort with, talk with, address): relating to or like a sermon.

"**Homiletic** language, if not restrained by compassion and humility, can appear as browbeating."

HYPERDULIA (HY-puhr-doo-LY-uh, HY-puhr-doo-LEE-uh): *n.* from Greek *hyper* (over, above) and Medieval Latin *dulia*, from Late Greek *douleia* (service, work done, business), from Greek *doulos* (slave): special veneration of the Virgin Mary.

"The **hyperdulia** given to the Virgin Mary reflects her exalted position within Roman Catholicism."

LAODICEAN (lay-AHD-uh-SEE-in): *adj.* from *Laodicea*, ancient city in Asia Minor whose Christian inhabitants were known for their lukewarm attitude toward their faith: lukewarm or indifferent in religion or politics.

"The minister held that the New Testament calls for unequivocal acceptance of faith and rejects **Laodicean** attitudes."

LATRIA (luh-TRY-uh): *n.* from Greek *latreia*; akin to Greek *latron* (pay, hire): in Roman Catholicism, the supreme homage that is given to God alone.

"The Roman Catholic priest asserted that Roman Catholics don't give the Virgin Mary the worship—the **latria**—that is due only to God; rather they venerate her, recognizing her special role in salvation."

MANICHEAN (man-un-KEE-uh): *adj.* from Late Latin *Manichaeus* (member of the Manchean sect), from Late Greek *Manichaios*, from *Manichaios* (Manes), a Persian sage who founded the sect and who died about 276 CE: a belief in a stark and completely unambiguous conflict between good and evil, with no shades of gray.

"The theology professor asserted that he rejected **Manichean** views as oversimplifying the moral life, which can involve making choices that involve good mixed with evil."

MARTEXT (MAHR-tekst): *n.* from English *mar* and *text*: a blundering preacher, especially one who stumbles through a sermon.

"The **martext** was so confused about the Bible and so halting in his sermon that he was fired."

NULLIFIDIAN (nuhl-uh-FID-ee-uhn): *n.* from Latin *nullus* (not, none, no) and *fides* (faith): a religious skeptic or disbeliever.

"Although Karl Marx was a **nullifidian** who regarded religious faith as often defending social and economic inequalities, he had an unwavering faith in an inevitable proletarian revolution."

PATEN (PAT-uhn): *n.* a plate made of precious metal used for bread in celebrating the Eucharist.

"The **paten** that was used during the church service was made of silver."

PISTOLOGY (pi-STAHL-uh-jee): *n.* from Greek *pistis* (faith): the branch of theology dealing with faith.

"When the philosopher of science was asked what he thought of faith, he answered that his fields are philosophy and science, not **pistology**."

PORNEROLOGY (PAHN-nuh-**RAHL**-uh-jee): *n.* from Greek *ponēros* (evil): in theology, the study of evil.

"Theologically, **pornerology** is concerned with not only sin but also natural or physical evil, such as the harm caused by hurricanes and tsunamis."

PSILANTHROPIST (sy-LAN-throh-pist): *n.* from Late Greek *psilanthrōpos* (merely human): one who believes that Christ was a mere man.

"Thomas Jefferson was a **psilanthropist** who accepted many of Jesus' ethical teachings but who believed that Jesus was fully human."

RECUSANT (REK-yuh-zuhnt, ri-KYOO-zuhnt): *n.* from Latin *recusant-*, *recusans*, present participle of *recusare* (to object to, refuse): (i) a Roman Catholic refusing to attend the services of the Church of England; (ii) a nonconformist.

"Years ago, when there was less religious freedom in England, **recusants** were not well regarded for refusing to attend religious services in the official state church."

SABBATARIAN: *n.* one who strictly observes the Sabbath.

"Jewish **Sabbatarians** will hire non-Jews to perform services forbidden to Jews on the Sabbath, such as turning lights on and off."

SACERDOTALISM (SAS-uhr-**DOH**-tuhl-IZ-uhm): *n.* from Latin *sacerdos* (priest): the belief that authorized priests are necessary mediators between God and people.

"Lutherans reject **sacerdotalism** and believe instead in the priesthood of individual believers."

SERMUNCLE: *n.* a short sermon.

"A churchgoer insulted the priest by insisting on a **sermuncle** rather than a 'long-winded sermon.'"

SOLIFIDIAN (sahl-uh-FID-ee-uhn): *n.* from Latin *solus* (alone) and *fides* (faith): a person who maintains that faith alone, without good works, is all that is necessary for salvation.

"The Protestant minister was a **solifidian** who claimed that faith in Christ is both necessary and sufficient for salvation."

TEREFAH (tuh-RAY-fuh): *n.* from Hebrew *terēphāh*, from *tāraph* (to tear, rend): (i) the meat of animals killed accidentally or by beasts of prey and forbidden to the Israelites as food; (ii) a food, food product, or utensil that isn't ritually clean or prepared according to Jewish law and is therefore prohibited.

"Orthodox Jews are forbidden to eat pork, shellfish, and other **terefah**."

THEODICY (THEE-ahd-uh-see): *n.* from Greek *theos* (god) and *dikē* (right, judgment): a theological attempt to vindicate God's justice in the light of evil.

"Milton's *Paradise Lost* is largely a **theodicy** in the form of an epic, in which the poet tries to explain, among other things, the reason for evil."

THEOMACHIST (THEE-ahm-uh-kist): *n.* from Greek *theos* (god, God) and *machē* (battle): one who resists God or the gods or the divine will.

"The preacher warned that Satanists and other **theomachists** will pay for their rejection of God in an unquenchable fire."

THEOPHANY (thee-AHF-uh-nee): *n.* from Medieval Latin *theophania*, from Late Greek *theophaneia*, from Greek *theo-*, *theos* (god) and *-phaneia* (appearance, manifestation): an appearance of a god to a person.

"In the Hebrew scriptures, there are some **theophanies**, as when in Genesis 12:7–9, the Lord appears to Abraham on Abraham's arrival in the land God had promised to him and his descendants."

ZUCHETTO (zoo-KET-oh): *n.* the skullcap worn by Roman Catholic clergy.

"Within the Roman Catholic Church priests wear black **zuchetti**, bishops wear violet ones, and the Pope wears a white one."

~~~~~~~~~~~~~~~~~~~~~~~~~~~~~~~~~~~~~~~

ROADS

~~~~~~~~~~~~~~~~~~~~~~~~~~~~~~~~~~~~~~~

CORNICHE (kor-NEESH): *n.* from French *corniche* (cornice): a road alongside a cliff or steep slope, especially coastline.

"If you drive down Hawk's Nest on New York State Route 97, a tightly winding section of the road along the Delaware River, you'll be traveling on a **corniche**."

RUMBLE STRIP: *n.* a strip of corrugated pavement (as along the edge of a highway) that causes a rumbling sound when driven over to keep drivers awake.

"Donald's chauffeur would have fallen asleep on the highway had he not driven over a **rumble strip**."

~~~~~~~~~~~~~~~~~~~~~~~~~~~~~~~~~~~~~~~

SEX

~~~~~~~~~~~~~~~~~~~~~~~~~~~~~~~~~~~~~~~

EPICENE (EP-i-seen): *adj.* from Greek *epikoinos*, from *epi-* (upon) and *koinos* (common): (i) having characteristics of both sexes or no characteristics of either sex; (ii) effeminate.

"The rock star David Bowie and the actor Christopher Walken have **epicene** facial features, creating sexually ambiguous appearances."

FROTTEURISM (fraw-**TOHR**-IZ-uhm): *n.* from French *frotter* (to rub): rubbing one's body against another for sexual gratification, especially in a crowded conveyance, such as an elevator, train, or bus.

"The eccentric woman was so worried about **frotteurism** that she used suspenders to wear a car tire around her midsection when she rode the subway or bus."

PARTIALISM: *n.* a sexual fetish in which a person is aroused more by a nonsexual part of the body (such as a foot) than by genitalia.

"We didn't know about Mickey's **partialism** until we saw him visibly aroused by Minnie's feet."

SATYRIASIS (say-tuh-RY-uh-sis, sat-uh-RY-uh-sis): *n.* from Greek *satyr* (a mythological creature often portrayed chasing after nymphs) and English -*mania* (excessive desire): excessive sexual desire in a man.

"Tiger Woods was unfaithful to his wife so often that he was in treatment for **satyriasis**."

Sociology

ANOMIE (AN-uh-MEE): *n.* from Greek *anomia, anomiē* (lawlessness): (i) a state of society in which normative standards of conduct and belief have weakened or disappeared; (ii) a similar condition in an individual characterized by personal disorientation, anxiety, and social isolation.

"The philosopher W. T. Stace was worried that a widespread belief in cultural relativism would lead to a state of **anomie**, in which each individual would believe that he or she is the only moral authority."

Sounds

BRONTIDE (BRAHN-tyd): *n.* from Greek *bronte* (thunder): a low muffled sound like distant thunder heard in some seismic regions, especially along seacoasts and over lakes and believed to be caused by weak earth tremors.

"We weren't sure whether the sound we heard was a **brontide** or actual thunder."

CHIRR (CHUHR): *n.* the shrill harsh trilled and repetitive sound made by certain insects, especially grasshoppers and cicadas.

"Most grasshoppers produce **chirrs** by rubbing a row of pegs along the inside of their hind legs against the thickened forewings, though some grasshoppers produce **chirrs** by snapping their hind wings quickly as they fly, making a crackling sound."

STRIDULATE: *v.* to make a shrill grating, chirping, or hissing sound by rubbing body parts together, as crickets and some other insects do.

"We heard crickets **stridulating** at nightfall."

TINTINNABULAR (TIN-ti-**NAB**-yuh-luhr): *adj.* from Middle English, from Latin *tintinnabulum* (bell), *tintinnare* (to jingle): of or relating to bells or the ringing of bells.

"As soon as we heard the **tintinnabular** sounds, we noticed the man ringing the bell was from the Salvation Army."

SPEECH

APHTHONG (af-THAWNG): *n.* from Greek *a-* (without) and *pthongos* (sound): a letter or letters that are spelled in a word but not pronounced ("silent letters").

"The word *knight* contains an **aphthong** because its first letter isn't pronounced."

MICROPHONIA: *n.* a weak, hardly audible voice.

"Because of the professor's **microphonia**, many students arrived to class early to sit in the front."

PARASIGMATISM: *n.* from Greek *para* (beside, alongside of) and English *sigmatism* (faulty articulation of sibilants), from Greek *sigma* (the eighteenth letter of the Greek alphabet): the inability to pronounce the sound of *s*, substituting that sound with some other sound (such as that of *f*).

"The little boy with **parasigmatism** was unhappy when his English teacher asked him to pronounce the tongue twister, 'She sells seashells at the seashore.'"

SUPERNATURALISM

GOLEM (GO-luhm): *n.* from Yiddish *goylem*, from Hebrew *gōlem* (something shapeless): in Jewish folklore, an anthropomorphic being created from inanimate matter.

"One of the most famous narratives about a **golem** involves the chief rabbi of Prague who, according to legend, created a **golem** to defend a Jewish ghetto from anti-Jewish attacks (pogroms)."

GRIMOIRE (grim-WAHR): *n.* from French, alteration of *grammaire* (grammar): a book of black magic, used for invoking demons and spirits.

"Soon after Jane began wearing black, her mother found a **grimoire** in her room."

INVULTUATION (in-vuhl-tyoo-AY-shuhn): *n.* from Medieval Latin *invultuare* (to make a likeness): the making of a likeness, especially a waxen effigy of a person for witchcraft.

"When Janice's parents discovered their waxen effigies with pins stuck in them, they immediately reduced her phone time to show how seriously they regarded the **invultuation**.

REVENANT (REV-uh-nuhnt): *n.* from French *revenir* (to come back): one that returns after a long absence or death.

"Ghosts, vampires, and zombies, if they exist, can qualify as **revenants**."

TRANSVECTION (trans-VER-shuhn): *n.* the supernatural act of levitating, floating, or, more specifically, flying through the air in defiance of gravity.

"Witches in medieval Europe were often depicted as flying on broomsticks (*see* BESOM under "Games / Recreations / Sports") or on wild animals or other means of **transvection**."

THEATER

ANNIE OAKLEY: *n.* a free theater ticket.

"Because we were friendly with the play's producer, we received five **Annie Oakleys**."

APPLE BOX: *n.* a fourteen-inch by twenty-four-inch platform used to elevate a performer on stage.

"When Dustin Hoffman stood on the **apple box**, he seemed as tall as most of the other actors in the play."

BAD LAUGH: *n.* in theater, laughter from the audience at an inappropriate moment.

"When the audience laughed at the speech impediment of the actor who was playing a serious part, everyone on stage resented the **bad laugh**."

CLAQUE (KLAK): *n.* from French *claquer* (to clap, of imitative origin): a group of persons hired to applaud at a performance.

"The radio talk show host accused the president of hiring a **claque** to applaud a speech."

GALANTY SHOW (guh-LAN-tee): *n.* perhaps from Italian *galante* (gallant): an entertainment in which a story is told by using shadows or miniature figures thrown on a wall or screen.

"The children enjoyed the **galanty show**, especially when the shadow figures were socking each other."

PROMPTER: *n.* in the theater, one who assists actors in recalling lines while the show is in progress.

"One actor in the play had trouble recalling his lines but wasn't helped much by the **prompter**, who was drunk."

PROSCENIUM (pruh-SEE-nee-uhm): *n.* from Greek *proskēnion* (the front of the building forming the background for a dramatic performance, stage): the part of a theater stage that is in front of the curtain.

"Right before the curtain was to open for the show, a man walked onto the **proscenium** to tell us that the show would be fifteen minutes late."

RAKE: *n.* a slant or inclination of a stage.

"When we walked from the back of the stage to the front, we noticed the **rake**."

RUMBLE POT: *n.* in the theater, a receptacle in which boiling water and dry ice are mixed to create fog effects.

"Although some people think that fog effects require high-tech, all that is needed is a **rumble pot**."

SUPERNUMERARY (SOO-puhr-**NOO**-muh-RAYR-ee): *n.* an actor without a speaking part, as one who appears in a crowd scene.

"Melissa would earn extra money by appearing as a **supernumerary** in movies, as when she recently depicted a customer in a restaurant drinking coffee."

TORMENTOR: *n.* a curtain or piece of scene that prevents the audience from seeing into the wings.

"The audience had a good chuckle when the **tormentor** fell down and revealed two stagehands necking."

Tobacco / Smoking

AMBEER (AM-beer): *n.* probably from *amber*, from its color: tobacco juice.

"When Thelma Lou kissed Barney, she tasted the **ambeer** from his chewing tobacco."

COMB: *n.* in a matchbook, the match stems together.

"We knew that the matchbook had been used because we saw several match stems missing from the **comb**."

MUNDUNGUS: *n.* from Spanish *mondongo* (tripe): tobacco with an offensive smell.

"When the gym teacher smelled an offensive odor from the boys' bathroom, he entered and found the source of the **mundungus**."

QUIFF: *n.* a puff of tobacco smoke.

"As soon as we entered the bar, some drinker decided to smoke, and we smelled a **quiff**."

SADDLE: *n.* the rounded part ("spine") on the top of a matchbook.

"The **saddle** of the matchbook was so well worn from use that the front cover of the book was about to come off."

STRIKER: *n.* the strip on a matchbook that lights the matches.

"When the **striker** was wet, we couldn't use it to light the matches."

TOOLS

CHATTER MARK: *n.* in machine tools, a rib-like marking on wood or metal by a vibrating tool, including an irregular surface flaw produced by a grinding wheel out of alignment or a regular mark produced by turning a long piece on a lathe.

"Because of the irregularity of the **chatter mark** on the wood, we thought that a wheel was out of alignment."

CRAMP: *n.* a clamp for holding pieces of wood together while they are glued.

"Our assistant needed to find the appropriate glue to apply to the pieces of wood before using the **cramp**."

CROWN: *n.* the horizontal part of a staple.

"A staple remover grabs the **crown** of a staple to remove it from a sheet of paper."

DIBBLE: *n.* a pointed gardening tool for boring holes for plants, seeds, or bulbs.

"We used **dibbles** to dig holes for the bulbs."

DUFFEL: *n.* from Dutch *duffel*, from *Duffel* (town near Antwerp, Belgium): transportable personal belongings, equipment, and supplies.

"The SUV carrying students back to West Point bulged with people, suitcases, and various **duffel**."

EYE: *n.* a hole in the head of an ax or hammer that receives the handle.

"We needed to apply some glue to the handle of the ax before reinserting it into the **eye** of the head."

FID: *n.* a sharp-pointed tool with a handle to do such jobs as making holes in leather.

"We used a **fid** to make an additional hole in the belt."

FLANG: *n.* a double-pointed miner's pick, which is also known as a *beele*.

"The miner's **flang** needed to be sharpened because it had been dulled from its almost constant use."

GRAB: *n.* the business end of a crane.

"The crane's **grab** picked up the car as if it were picking up a feather."

KERF (KURF): *n.* from Old English *cyrf* (a cutting): a slit or notch made by a cutting tool, such as a saw or an ax.

"The carpenter was careful to make the **kerf** through the wood as straight as possible."

LEG: *n.* one of the two vertical parts of a staple.

"Each staple has two **legs**, which are flattened once the staple is used."

NORIA: *n.* a waterwheel with attached buckets used to raise and deposit water, especially for irrigation.

"Some **norias** will lift water from rivers to small aqueducts at the top of the wheel."

PEAVEY: *n.* from Joseph *Peavey*, a Maine blacksmith: a lumberjack's tool consisting of a pole five to six feet in length fitted with a steel pike and an adjustable steel hook at the end.

"Lumberjacks use **peaveys** to turn and maneuver logs."

PEEN: *n.* the part of a hammerhead opposite the flat striking surface.

"The **peen** of a hammer, often rounded or wedge-shaped, is used for bending and shaping."

POLL: *n.* the broad or flat end of a hammer or similar tool.

"The nail-removing claw is at a top portion of the hammerhead between the **poll** and the handle."

SNATH: *n.* the handle of a scythe.

"We asked the young man to wear gloves while holding the **snath** to avoid blisters and calluses when using the scythe."

UTENSILS

KNORK: *n.* an eating utensil (*see* SPORK) combining the function of a knife and a fork.

"Typically, one or both of the outer edges of a **knork** are sharpened to allow the user to cut food."

RUNCIBLE (RUN-si-buhl): *n.* from Edward Lear, who wrote the poem "The Owl and the Pussycat," which contains "a **runcible** spoon": a combination of fork, spoon, and sometimes knife.

"A **runcible spoon** (*see* SPORK) has three prongs, a spoon-like receptacle, and a sharp edge for cutting."

SPORK: *n.* an eating utensil combining the functions and appearance of a spoon and a fork.

"I recall receiving plastic **sporks** at KFC restaurants, sparing people the need to use both spoons and forks."

TANG: *n.* the part of a knife blade that extends into the handle.

"We were told that the best knives have the longest **tangs** for balance."

TOBY: *n.* a drinking mug usually in the shape of a stout man wearing a three-cornered hat.

"It was difficult to be serious when we were talking to a man dressed as a clown drinking carrot juice out of a **toby**."

~~~~~~~~~~~~~~~~~~~~~~~

Vehicles

~~~~~~~~~~~~~~~~~~~~~~~

CREEPER: *n.* the stretcher with wheels that auto mechanics use to work underneath vehicles.

"The auto mechanic's body was so thick that when he lay down on the **creeper**, he could barely fit underneath the car he was working on."

GANTRY: *n.* in rocketry, a service tower that consists of a multistory frame that encloses a rocket at its launch pad and that contains elevators and staircases.

"The **gantry** enabled technicians to inspect, maintain, and adjust all parts of the rocket and was the means through which the astronauts entered the ship."

JEHU (JEE-hyoo, JEE-hoo): *n.* from a king of Israel who drove chariots furiously: a fast or reckless driver of a cab or coach.

"In Manhattan, cabdrivers have reputations as impatient **jehus** who are quick to speed even on cramped streets."

MARS LIGHT: *n.* the flashing light on an ambulance, fire truck, police cruiser, and railroad locomotive.

"**Mars lights** were originally developed by a Chicago firefighter who realized that the oscillating lights would benefit not only fire departments but also railroads."

ORNITHOPTER: *n.* from Greek *ornith-*, *ornis* (bird) and *pteron* (wing): an early flying machine with flapping wings.

"The first **ornithopters** capable of flight were constructed in France in the 1870s and had wings powered by gunpowder charges activating a pressure-sensing device."

PEDIDDLE: *n.* urban slang for a car with only one head-light on.

"The traveling game **Pediddle** requires players to be the first person to yell '**pediddle**' when seeing a car with only one lit headlight."

PENNY-FARTHING: *n.* from the name of the British coins penny and farthing (a quarter penny, much smaller than the penny): an old-fashioned bicycle with the big wheel in front and the tiny wheel in the rear.

"The **penny-farthing**, popular from about 1870 to 1890, was probably just called a 'bicycle' until nearly the end of its popularity to distinguish it from what was called a 'safety bicycle,' which became popular in the 1880s and which looked like modern bikes (before extra gears)."

SKIBOB: *n.* a vehicle for sliding downhill over snow.

"A **skibob** resembles a bicycle on skis."

TROLLEY POLE: *n.* a vertical pole of a bumper car.

"In old-fashioned bumper cars, contacts under the vehicle touch the floor while the **trolley pole** touches the ceiling, forming a complete circuit."

TURNTABLE: *n.* in firefighting, the platform and hydraulic motor that raises a ladder and turns it on a ladder truck.

"The **turntable** on which a fire truck ladder is mounted allows the ladder to pivot around a stable base, in turn allowing a much greater ladder length."

WHEEL GUARD: *n.* the small concrete or asphalt bars that one parks one's car wheels against in parking lots.

"Sammy quickly applied the brakes after he hit the **wheel guard** in the parking lot."

~~~~~~~~~~

VOICE

~~~~~~~~~~

BURR: *n.* a trilled avular \r\, produced by vibrating the uvula against the back of the tongue, as in the speech of Scotland and northern England.

"After an operation in which Heather's uvula was damaged, it was difficult for her to pronounce a **burr**."

CACHINNATE (KAK-i-nayt): *v.* from Latin *cachinnare* (to laugh aloud or immoderately): to laugh loudly or convulsively.

"The comedian was so funny, and we felt so unre-strained that we began to **cachinnate** for several minutes."

CONCATENATED SPEECH: *n.* recorded or synthesized words that have been spliced together to produce an an-swer or directed in a dialogue between a computer and a person.

"When we called the corporation, **concatenated speech** directed us through the voice mail."

ORTHOEPY (or-THOH-uh-pee, OR-thoh-ep-EE): *n.* from Greek *orth-*, *orthos* (straight, correct, right) and *-epeia*, *epos* (word, speech): the study of pronunciation, especially a description of customary pronunciation.

"It is ironic, though perhaps liberating, that **orthoepy**, which is supposed to describe customary pronunciation, has a name with two acceptable pronunciations."

RHINOPHONIA (RY-nuh-**FOH**-nee-uh): *n.* from Greek *rhino-*, *rhis*, *rhinos* (nose, snout) and *-phonia*, *phone* (sound, voice): extreme nasal sound in the voice.

"Bill was called Ducky because of his **rhinophonia**."

SCHESIS (SKEE-suhs): *n.* from Greek *schein* (to have, hold): a figure of speech in which a person mocks an adversary's accent or style of speaking to discredit the per-son or the person's positions.

"The radio talk show host Rush Limbaugh likes to use **schesis** when he criticizes the positions of political adversaries."

SLURVIAN: *n.* speech characterized by slurring.

"The boy didn't speak standard American English but **slurvian**, peppered with *gimme*, *c'mon*, and *d'ju*."

STEM-WINDER: *n.* from the superiority of the stem-winding watch over the older key-wound watch: a stirring speech.

"After the president delivered a **stem-winder**, his approval rating went up by five points."

VAGITUS (vuh-JY-tus): *n.* from Latin *vagire* (to cry): the first cry of a newborn child.

"After the physician slapped the baby on her butt, we heard the baby's **vagitus**."

VERBIGERATE (vur-BIJ-ur-ayt): *n.* from Latin *verbigeratus*, past participle of *verbigerare* (to talk): to repeat a word or sentence obsessively and meaninglessly, especially as a symptom of a psychiatric disorder.

"The disoriented man wouldn't engage in a conversation but would instead repeat certain phrases, **verbigerating** for hours."

VOICE EXEMPLAR: *n.* in law, a recording of a person's voiced used as identification in a court proceeding.

"When the jurors heard the **voice exemplar**, they believed that the threatening phone call message did come from the defendant."

WRITING

ALLOGRAPH (**AL**-uh-**GRAF**): *n.* from Greek *allos* (other) and *-graph* (writing): a signature made by one person for another.

"The administrative assistant was authorized to produce the **allograph** for her boss."

GRIFFONAGE (GREE-fun-**NAHZH**, GRI-fuh-**NAHZH**): *n.* from Middle French *grifouner* (to scribble): sloppy or illegible handwriting.

"The physician's **griffonage** was so bad that the pharmacist was unsure about the strength of the prescription."

OBELIZE: *v.* to designate or annotate with an obelus (÷), especially to mark the beginning of a passage in ancient manuscripts thought possibly corrupt or spurious.

"Editors have **obelized** some ancient manuscripts, indicating that they doubted their authenticity."

OPISTHOGRAPHY (AHP-is-**THAWG**-ruh-fee): *n.* from Greek *opisthen*, *opithen* (behind, in the rear) and *-graphos* (writing): a writing upon the back of anything, as upon parchment or upon the back of a sheet of paper already written on one side.

"On bank checks, **opisthography** is normal when people endorse the checks."

PARAPH (PAR-uhf, puh-RAF): *n.* from French *paraffe* (abbreviated signature), from Medieval Latin *paraphus* (paragraph sign), short for *paragraphus* (paragraph): a flourish made at the end of a signature, usually to prevent forgery.

"The rich man's highly intricate **paraph** made it difficult to forge his signature."

STEGANOGRAPHY (ste-guh-NAHG-ruh-fee): *n.* from Greek *stegein* (to cover) and *-graphy* (writing): the art of writing hidden messages in such a way that no one, except the senders and the intended recipients, suspects even the existence of the message, much less its content.

"Cryptography differs from **steganography** because the former encrypts a message, whereas the latter hides it altogether, as when absorbing it in a selective reading of shopping lists, in variable sizes of letters (such as the dot of the letter *i*), or in invisible ink between the visible lines of private letters."

SELECTED BIBLIOGRAPHY

The American Heritage Dictionary of the English Language. 3rd ed. Boston: Houghton Mifflin, 1992.

Berent, Irwin M., and Rod L. Evans. *More Weird Words.* New York: Berkley Books, 1995.

Berent, Irwin M., and Rod L. Evans. *Weird Words.* New York: Berkley Books, 1995.

Bernstein, Theodore. *The Careful Writer: A Modern Guide to English Usage.* New York: Atheneum, 1973.

Bowler, Peter. *The Superior Person's Book of Words.* New York: Dell Laurel, 1982.

Bowler, Peter. *The Superior Person's Second Book of Weird and Wondrous Words.* Boston: Godine, 1992.

Brown, Roland Wilbur. *Composition of Scientific Words: A Manual of Methods and a Lexicon of Materials for the Practice of Logotechnics.* Washington, DC: Smithsonian Institution Press, 1956.

Copeland, Robert, ed. *Webster's Sports Dictionary.* Springfield, MA: Merriam, 1976.

Danziger, Danny, and Mark McCrum. *The Whatchamacallit: Those Everyday Objects You Just Can't Name (and Things You Think You Know About But Don't).* New York: Hyperion, 2009.

The Diagram Group. *The Dictionary of Unfamiliar Words.* New York: Skyhorse, 2008.

Dickson, Paul. *Dickson's Word Treasury: A Connoisseur's Collection of Old and New, Weird and Wonderful, Useful and Outlandish Words.* New York: Wiley, 1992.

Ehrlich, Eugene. *The Highly Selective Dictionary of Golden Adjectives for the Extraordinarily Literate.* New York: HarperCollins, 2002.

Elster, Charles Harrington. *There's a Word for It!: A Grandiloquent Guide to Life*. New York: Scribner, 1996.

Evans, Rod L. *The Gilded Tongue*. Cincinnati, OH: Writer's Digest Books, 2006.

Evans, Rod L., and Irwin M. Berent. *Getting Your Words' Worth: Discovering and Enjoying Phantonyms, Gramograms, Anagrams, and Other Fascinating Word Phenomenon*. New York: Warner Books, 1993.

Fowler, W. *A Dictionary of Modern English Usage*. Scranton, PA: Hadden Craftsman, 1944.

Garg, Ann, and Stuti Garg. *A Word a Day: A Romp Through Some of the Most Unusual and Intriguing Words in English*. Hoboken, NJ: Wiley, 2003.

Gause, John T. *The Complete University Word Hunter*. New York: Crowell, 1967.

Grambs, David. *The Describer's Dictionary*. New York: Norton, 1993.

Grambs, David. *The Endangered English Dictionary: Bodacious Words Your Dictionary Forgot*. New York: Norton, 1994.

Handford, S. A., and Mary Herberg. *Langenscheidt's Shorter Latin Dictionary*. Berlin, 1966.

Heifetz, Josepha (Mrs. Byrne). *Mrs. Byrne's Dictionary of Unusual, Obscure, and Preposterous Words*. Expanded ed. Secaucus, NJ: Card, 1994.

Hill, Robert, ed. *A Dictionary of Difficult Words*. Rev. ed. New York: Gramercy, 1990.

Hunsberger, I. Moyer. *The Quintessential Dictionary*. New York: Hart, 1978.

Lederer, Richard. *Adventurers of a Verbivore*. New York: Pocket Books, 1994.

Lederer, Richard. *Crazy English: The Ultimate Joy Ride Through Our Language*. New York: Pocket Books, 1989.

Lederer, Richard. *The Play of Words: Fun & Games for Language Lovers*. New York: Pocket Books, 1990.

McCutcheon, Marc. *Descriptionary: A Thematic Dictionary*. New York: Facts on File, 1992.

McKean, Erin, ed. *Weird and Wonderful Words*. New York: Oxford University Press, 2002.

Novobatzky, Peter, and Ammon Shea. *Depraved English*. New York: St. Martin's Press, 1999.

Partridge, Eric. *Origins: A Short Etymological Dictionary of Modern English*. New York: Greenwich House, 1983.

Partridge, Eric. *Usage and Abusage*. Middlesex, UK: Penguin, 1974.

Paxson, William C. *The New American Dictionary of Confusing Words*. New York: Signet, 1990.

Rocke, Russell. *The Grandiloquent Dictionary*. Englewood Cliff, NJ: Prentice-Hall, 1972.

Saussy, George Stone III. *The Oxter English Dictionary: Uncommon Words Used by Uncommonly Good Writers*. New York: Facts on File, 1984.

Urdang, Laurence, ed. *Modifiers*. Detroit: Gale Research, 1982.

Urdang, Laurence. *The New York Times Everyday Reader's Dictionary of Misunderstood, Misused, and Mispronounced Words*. New York: Quadrangle/The New York Times, 1972.

Webster's Third New International Dictionary of the English Language. Unabridged. Springfield, MA: Merriam, 1971.

Westley, Miles. *The Bibliophile's Dictionary*. Cincinnati, OH: Writer's Digest Books, 2005.